MICHAEL M. MISKULIN

A FRAMEWORK FOR HOA MANAGEMENT

BEST PRACTICES FOR SUCCESS

LEADING ORDER SOLUTIONS

A Framework for HOA Management

Best Practices For Success

Copyright © 2012 Leading Order Solutions Inc.

Port Chester, NY 10573

Photo Credits: Front- Catalano, Miskulin, Rear- Catalano

ISBN 978-0-9885686-0-0 Softcover
ISBN 978-0-9885686-1-7 Hardcover
ISBN 978-0-9885686-2-4 Kindle
ISBN 978-0-9885686-3-1 ePub

PUBLISHED BY LEADING ORDER SOLUTIONS
First printing, November 2012

Typeset using LaTeX in the Tufte-LaTeX style. Source style definitions and classes are available at: TUFTE-LATEX.GOOGLECODE.COM

Printed in the United States of America on acid and lignin free paper

Contents

6

List of Figures

Forward

The genesis for *A Framework for HOA Management* was the author's three years as president of a mid-sized HOA of about 200 residents with an annual budget of $500,000. Over the prior fifteen years, I was asked numerous times to join the board but declined, instead helping now and then with the ad-hoc project of the moment. In 2008, a large project had begun to go awry, and many homeowners were angry and nervous about the future of the association. I was roped into co-leading a group of "rebels" who, somehow, succeeded in replacing the entire ruling "junta" of seven, mostly long time, board members. As circumstance would have it, I was elected president by the other board members. Thus began a tumultuous three years of rule changes, contractor replacement, capital projects and the replacement of our management agent of the prior two decades.

Looking back, it would have been a great help to have had some resource available which explained how best to run a board meeting, the many ins and outs of pools, siding, paint, drainage, etc., and most importantly, how to plan for the future. Besides helping to avoid a number of mistakes, such a book could have reduced the stress level on myself as well as the entire board.

After three very busy years, I felt the time was right to open up a place on the board for another member of the community and turn over the day-to-day management of the association to one of my fellow board members. The board had completed the reforms and projects I believed were most important, and I would now return to "civilian" life. In the subsequent months, the notion of writing a book on the subject of HOA management went from just a wild, passing thought to the volume in your hands today.

Of course, I had help along the way and while many have offered comments and suggestions, I would like to thank, in particular, Kevin for providing both the impetus to run for the board as well as his work in setting a lasting basis for the better governance of our association; Connie for enduring my many requests for her opinion on both content and presentation; Ronnie for her patience copy editing; and Tom for his assistance with both the editing and marketing of *A Framework for HOA Management.*

Finally, I would like to thank my father for his love, support and dedication, without which this work would never have been possible.

November 2012

Preface

The audience for *A Framework for HOA Management* is any homeowner or resident who is currently on the board of directors of their homeowners association (HOA), is considering joining the board, or just wishes to be better informed on the various issues facing every HOA so that they can ask pertinent questions of the property manager or board members. The text is largely non-technical, and explanations are given where necessary.

The goal of *A Framework for HOA Management* is to provide the reader with the tools needed to effectively manage an HOA, including both guidance on establishing a sound physical plant and instruction on governance, oversight and planning. By the end of the book, the reader will be able to formulate a credible and efficacious response to any issue confronting their HOA.

HOAs come in a wide variety of sizes, both in terms of units and the property on which they are situated. In addition, governing documents can vary from state to state, as well as by the size of the association. Very large associations may even have multiple boards of directors. As it would be extremely difficult to address every situation, this book instead focuses on HOAs of 25 to 250 units on property of 5 to 40 acres.

HOAs of that size generally do not have a property manager assigned exclusively to their association, as do many of the very large associations, nor do they have full-time maintenance employees. The board is expected to have responsibilities beyond the landscaping of the property that may include limited maintenance of deeded homeowner property, such as shingles, gutters or paint.

A Framework for HOA Management begins with a look at the structure of a typical board of directors, the roles and responsibilities of the officers and continues to the discussion of the association's legal representation.

For new board members in particular, board meetings can be a nerve wracking experience. The chapter on meetings covers topics, such as when to schedule meetings, the merits of public versus closed sessions, general procedures to follow to have a productive meeting and how to handle large projects.

A subject that can cause much anguish for boards, homeowner relations, is covered next. How board members interact with the homeowners and how the board is perceived by them can make the difference between constant battles between the board and groups of homeowners or a mutually supportive relationship. Rules and regulations are another area that can cause problems for a board. The suggestions made in both of these chapters have been found to work well in practice, though their implementation may require a leap of faith and change in attitude by some board members.

The topic of insurance is often given only fleeting consideration by the board of directors, usually at the time the association's corporate policies are renewed. Going beyond specific items of concern in the association's own policies, this chapter covers how the association is also intertwined with the individual homeowners' insurance.

A significant focus of any board are issues concerning the common grounds. The property chapter is the most significant of the book and covers a very diverse range of topics – from pool operations to landscaping, to the color of fire hydrants. Essential details and common pitfalls are discussed at length in order to give board members a leg up on topics they may not be familiar and to better detect when a property manager or contractor is attempting to take advantage of their expected naivety. Common projects, such as painting the homes, drainage repair, lighting, and paving are discussed.

Contractors are frequent visitors to any association, whether to do landscaping each week or to work on a capital project. The contracting chapter ties together a number of issues that are raised in other chapters. In addition, there is a discussion of how to handle the situation when things go wrong.

Except for the rare self-managed association, all HOAs employ the services of a property management company. The chapter on the management agent begins with a discussion of terms which are common to most property management contracts, with a translation to practical, real world terms. Discussed next are solutions to the typical problems every board will encounter with both the property manager assigned to the property and the supporting staff within the management agency. As sometimes the problems run too deep to repair, there is an in depth examination of the procedures to follow when searching for a new management agent, as well as the considerations necessary for a smooth transition.

Although the treasurer and president are the most involved with the finances of the association, the entire board should be familiar with the budgeting process. The budgeting chapter covers the basics of generating the annual operating budget and then extends the conversation to the very important topic of capital budgeting. That discussion, by necessity, involves the entire board.

Rounding out the book are four appendices. Appendix A includes a number of sample policies and protocols. These should be modified and adopted by any association that does not already have similar provisions in place. Appendix B contains the key sections of a typical financial report that is sent to board members every month by the management agent. Appendix C is a discussion of the planning necessary for a successful painting project, complete with example Gantt charts; painting is often one of the largest capital projects a board will undertake. This example can also serve as a framework for other projects. Finally, Appendix D contains information related to electronic communications and how to get the board "on-line" while also avoiding potential legal and other liabilities.

A BRIEF NOTE ON TERMINOLOGY:

The terms "property manager" and "management agent" are often used interchangeably. In this book, however, the management agent (or "management agency") is defined as the firm which employs the property manager and other support staff, such as accountants, to provide services to the association. The property manager is the individual who comes to the property, interacts with the board, and handles most, though not necessarily all, management functions.

The Structure Of The Board

Roles and Responsibilities

MEMBERSHIP IN THE BOARD OF DIRECTORS should not be viewed as joining a club – the title "board member" comes with specific legal obligations that cannot be ignored. Every home-owner or condominium association is formally organized as either a "C corporation" or LLC. As such, board members must pay attention to things which often may seem like formalities but are in fact procedures put in place to protect both the board and the members of the association from financial and legal harm.

The primary source of information on this subject is the bylaws of the association. Contained within that document is, at a minimum, information related to the election of board members, replacement and removal of board members, selection of officers of the association, responsibilities of the officers, and meeting requirements. Board members should review this ma-terial carefully and understand that the bylaws are not a guide that is subject to their interpretation as may be convenient at any particular time. These are the rules of a corporation and must be followed. Failure to follow these rules may open indi-vidual members, the entire board, and possibly the association to a lawsuit.

A common problem at board meetings is that board members

do not always have the necessary information organized and on hand. When questions about the homeowners' agreement come up, are all board members struggling to read from the same copy? Did any even remember to bring a copy to the meeting? The same can be said about rules, regulations and policies put in place by the current board and its predecessors. Not having this type of information on-hand can grind a meeting to a halt or result in decisions being made based on speculation or memory.

A better approach is to create a set of document binders to hold copies of the bylaws, homeowners' agreement, policy statements, rules and regulations, financial reports and the many other documents which pass by the board. Officers, such as the treasurer, may have a special section containing recent bank statements and audit papers. Besides keeping information at the finger tips, the binders can be passed on to new members as others step down. A well kept binder provides continuity and allows the new member to get up to speed far quicker and with less need for detailed explanations that can slow down a board meeting.

Officers

The board must be clear on the roles, rights and responsibilities of the officers of the corporation. Much animosity and contention can occur when some board members feel the officers are not including them (rightly or wrongly) in decision making or are keeping them in the dark by not immediately notifying them of new events or information. There is a great tendency for other board members, non-officers in particular, to second guess minor decisions made by the president. Likewise, some will feel slighted if every conversation an officer has with the management agency, a vendor or a homeowner is not immediately reported to the entire board, even though many property managers prefer to interact with only one or two board members in-between meetings to minimize receiving conflicting instructions.

When the bylaws articulate specific responsibilities of the president and other officers (for instance, overseeing day-to-day operation of the association), the board should take a few minutes after the annual election, ideally before new officers are selected (if chosen by the board), to review these responsibilities and clear the air of exactly what the officers can and cannot do without full board approval, what reporting requirements are acceptable, etc. When information to and from the agent flows through only one or two officers, the board should also establish parameters for what types of events and information require the notification of the full board.

If the bylaws do not delineate such responsibilities, all the more reason why the board must establish such ground rules at an early stage. After this discussion, some members may no longer wish to be an officer as they would feel either unnecessarily constrained or burdened by the ground rules. Having this talk at the outset will result in fewer misunderstandings and squabbles later on.

The President

The president is the board member with primary responsibility for the day-to-day operations of the association and is the association's primary contact with the property manager, the attorney and possibly some of the contractors. In the normal course of work, the property manager will often be faced with multiple alternatives to solve a problem and may contact the president to have a choice "blessed" before acting or to ask for an opinion of the competing solutions. Similarly, the president will often contact the property manager with new work items, such as repair or information requests. Though it is helpful if the president and property manager are on good personal terms, what is most important is that they work well with one other.

Guidelines and parameters should be established early on

concerning call backs, status updates, information requests and the like. Some property managers will lean heavily on the president to be the gatekeeper and keep the rest of the board out of their hair. Others have no problem dealing with multiple board members, or should the board so decide, the delegation of areas of responsibility to specific board members. Flowing the other way, some property managers prefer that board members only speak with them and not other employees of the management agency. Others will have no issue with the president contacting the accounting department directly or speaking with an administrative assistant to request a copy of a report.

If the board is uncomfortable with the arrangements the property manager prefers, as the client they should request the terms be adjusted more to their liking. Remember, though, that some policies may be set company wide by the property manager's superiors, and the board should be prepared to speak with them if it does not think it can operate well under those terms.

The president may find it beneficial and perhaps necessary to have some interaction with the association's major contractors, such as the landscaper or pool service company. Always remember that even though these contractors are directed primarily by the property manager, that does not mean the direction they receive is adequate or proper. In order for the landscaper to keep the association's business, they must make the property look not just presentable, but beautiful. However, if the property manager says to skip lawn treatments or other work (perhaps to offset an over budget item elsewhere), then the landscaper's standing is put at risk. Remember, all of these firms work for the association, not the management agency. The president must be available to the contractors to hear their concerns and if necessary, act to make changes to alleviate them. There may also be situations when a contractor is having problems with a homeowner or resident but does not wish to involve the management agency for fear of inflaming an already difficult situation. Again, the contractor should speak directly with the president about any concerns.

The president is also responsible for setting the agenda of the board meetings and may do this alone or in conjunction with the property manager. In addition, the president will lead the discussions at the meetings and acts as moderator when necessary. The president needs to have fairly good knowledge of where other board members stand on the meeting agenda items prior to opening any discussions, especially if there may be a vote on a course of action or a contract proposal. With this knowledge, the president is better able to guide the board through its discussions without getting too bogged down in potentially contentious issues or worse, bringing an action to vote that is unlikely to pass or has only weak backing.

One of the most difficult tasks of the presidency is to manage the politics and individual agendas of the board of directors; it can be a great challenge to prevent the board from developing into factions or cliques. Further complicating the job can be the bad behavior of the spouses and children of board members. At best, this situation can create uncomfortable feelings and at worst, may poison the atmosphere at all future meetings and result in the ostracization of that board member. The same situation can occur when a board member becomes fixated with violations of the parking, pet or other regulations. As well as being tiresome to listen to, this type of board vigilantism may be difficult for the property manager too. They rightly fear homeowner backlash at the appearance of a board member using a position of power to engage in personal vendettas.

Dealing with these types of political issues is ultimately very wearing and can consume more of the president's time than the real work of leading the management of the association. The president is advised not to allow issues with a board member's children, spouse or personal conduct to go unchecked. The sooner the offending board member is told the situation is unacceptable, the better and the less likely there will be any resentment that precludes a good working relationship with the other board members, the property manager and the residents of the association.

The Vice President

The role of the vice president is often ill defined by the bylaws. Usually, the only requirement of the position is that the vice president assume the responsibilities of the president if they are no longer able to discharge their duties. This is usually inter-preted to mean some kind of physical calamity has incapacitated the president, although in the case of a homeowners associa-tion, it could simply be that the president is out of town on a business trip. First hand, on-site observation is often necessary to understand the extent of a problem, and thus the president must delegate much, if not all, authority to the vice president until their return.

If the president steps down from their position or even the board entirely, the vice president will assume that role until such time as the full board meets to nominate and elect a new president. If the election of officers is done at the annual meeting by the direct vote of the homeowners, the bylaws will likely automatically elevate the vice president to the presidency for the remainder of the term.

Because of the next in line nature of the office, the president should try to keep the vice president aware of any pending issues which have not been brought before the entire board. This includes private discussions which could be important to know were the vice president to take charge unexpectedly. Even though it is critical to avoid a "co-presidency," it remains good practice for the president to speak with the vice president regularly and as otherwise necessary between board meetings.

Outside of emergency situations, this office is whatever the vice president, the president and other officers wish it to be. The president may delegate special projects, interaction with specific contractors or the handling of certain meetings to the vice president. However, those types of delegations can be made to other board members as well.

The Treasurer

The treasurer's primary duty is to ensure that the association is maintained in stable and good financial condition. The treasurer is usually the person who authorizes non-routine payments to contractors and the movement of funds among accounts. The treasurer will also invest excess funds of the association in a manner either defined by the bylaws or through general guidance from the entire board and management agency. A thorough review of the monthly financial statements prepared by the management agency is also the responsibility of the treasurer, as is working with the association's independent auditor to prepare financial and other statements to satisfy the many requirements placed upon the association by state and federal laws.

Taking those one by one, what does stable and good financial condition mean? Stability refers to the ability of the association to meet its obligations from month to month without the need of financial shenanigans, such as deferring contractor payments or other bills. Use of an overdraft facility should be a rarity, and like every family, the goal should be not to live paycheck to paycheck. If the association is consistently unable to pay its routine bills, either the budget has significantly underestimated regular expenses or the monthly common charge is too low. Even though it is possible for arrearages to result in a shortfall in total revenue, if this causes the association to run out of funds every month, then the budget was too tight and too little attention was paid to past and expected arrearages.

Good financial condition extends the concept of stability to the longer term. Does the association have the funds necessary to meet its capital obligations? Does a capital plan exist? Does the association have reserves of at least 10% of its expected annual outlays? Since 2009, mortgage lending standards have tightened significantly. At the same time, federally guaranteed lending agencies, like Fannie Mae, placed this reserve requirement on HOA and condominium loans they purchase from mortgage originators. As lending institutions sell the vast majority of loans they originate to Fannie Mae (FNMA) or Freddie Mac (FHLMC), homeowners wishing to move may not find a buyer for their units unless the new reserve requirement has been met by the association.

The treasurer needs to be the one who takes the punch bowl away from the other board members when spending looks to exceed the budget or reserve funds are depleted. Reserves should not be used to finance the daily operations of the association or superfluous projects.

The treasurer must also make sure that the association maintains the proper mix of bank and investment accounts. As a result, the treasurer must be on every signature card (as must the president and a senior officer of the management agency). The choice of accounts to maintain becomes more complex as the funds held grow. At a minimum, the association should maintain one operating and one reserve account at a reputable bank.

Often, the management agency will have an arrangement with a particular bank that simplifies operations they make on the association's behalf. However, do not feel compelled to use the bank they suggest. If the management agency covers a wide geographic area, the bank may be far away from the property which can be an inconvenience if signature cards or other papers must be signed or changed. Also, the bank may not have terms as favorable as others available to the association. Thus, it is up to the treasurer to fully review the situation and recommend to the entire board the bank(s) that offer the association the best business relationship. Please remember the last phrase: business relationship.

Although one operating account and one reserve account are a good starting point (and may be all that is needed for a very small association), consideration also must be given to the expected size of the reserve account and whether it is prudent to maintain additional reserve accounts at other banks or even to have an account with a brokerage. If the association expects to make use of a capital plan and future funds reserved will be sizable (over $100,000), additional reserve accounts are called for. One reason is FDIC insurance limits. Although the insured limits were raised during the financial crisis of 2008–2009, it is not certain for how long those higher limits will remain in place, and they may revert to $100,000.

Further, because funds may be unavailable during the resolution of a crisis at a bank, it is best not to keep all of the funds at one institution. A good fall back is to maintain at least one additional account funded with a minimum of one month's typical operating needs. The treasurer should also look to the quality, not size, of the financial institution. Large money center banks may offer many services that a smaller institution will not, but the large bank may have a far weaker balance sheet and consequently a higher risk of failure.

At an association that expects to have an ongoing need for capital projects, the treasurer definitely should consider opening multiple reserve accounts and fund them "short," "medium," and "long," to match the duration until the start of the projects, or open specific accounts for each project. *Depending on the association's location, it may even be legally mandated to do the latter.* An additional benefit of using multiple accounts is that homeowners will have a far better sense of where their money is and how the balances are changing over time. Red flags will be raised if a board draws down a long term account without performing the work the account was meant to fund. Likewise, shifts among the accounts with no explanation will raise eyebrows and questions at the next homeowners meeting.

Some associations may have restrictions in their homeowners' agreement or bylaws that specify what are acceptable investments, and if so, the board may not deviate from that list. Though the investment of reserve funds into equities is *not* recommended, it may be necessary to have a brokerage account if the treasurer feels the best investment returns will come from medium or long term government obligations (e.g., a five year treasury note) as these products are not normally available through a bank. The universe of CDs available for purchase from a brokerage is also greater. However, there may be annual maintenance fees that offset any additional interest earned or the increased investment flexibility this type of account may offer when compared with those available at a local or regional bank. In addition, investing in CDs is not without risk and because of their diversity, it is difficult for a non-specialist to know which issuers to avoid.

Also, were a broker-dealer to go under rapidly, as did Bear Stearns and Lehman Brothers, the association might find its reserve accounts are frozen for a considerable period of time (This is to allow bankruptcy courts to review financial records to establish that all funds were properly segregated before allowing any return of capital to clients.) This could prove devastating if a project were under way for which those funds are needed. Although most firms are good about segregating customer and firm capital, there have been cases where monies which belonged to the clients were used by the broker-dealer and subsequently lost. Brokerage accounts should only be considered when there is *truly a need for an alternative investment not available through more traditional routes.* For instance, US government obligations can be purchased without a broker via the Treasury Direct website after opening and funding an institutional account.

Earlier, the phrase business relationship was mentioned. This, too, should be factored into the decision making process. Even a new development must plan for future capital projects, and it is unlikely that any association will reserve 100% of the expected cost of each and every project. A loan is inevitable at some point, and that is when having existing banking relationships of more than passing duration will be to the association's benefit. If several reserve accounts are maintained with local or regional banks, the association will be in a good position when the time comes to take down a loan to complete a very large project. Instead of having just one bank to lean on, it may have three or four. This does not preclude the association from applying for a loan with an institution which they have had no prior dealings, but a previous history will improve the chances of a loan offer in the amount and on the terms it desires.

The Secretary

The secretary is the record keeper for the board. Minutes of meetings must be kept, distributed, approved and signed by the secretary. Notices related to the annual meeting, the counting of proxies and other similar tasks are the responsibility of the secretary and may also require a signature to be considered valid. In this regard, the secretary must be familiar with the requirements of the association's bylaws to ensure that its business is conducted in a legally binding manner. The property manager or other individual at the management agency should be familiar with the specific requirements in the state the association is located, and they should assist the secretary in fulfilling these duties, at the annual meeting in particular.

In some cases, the property manager will act as recorder at the board meetings and provide a written set of notes to the secretary for review and use as meeting minutes. If so, care should be taken that all relevant details of the meeting are included and that names, titles, amounts, unit numbers etc., are correct. The bylaws may or may not envision the post of assistant secretary. However, it is a good idea to have another board member designated as such, even if informally, in case the secretary is unable to attend a meeting. Also, when the board designates certain members to form a subcommittee, minutes of those committee meetings should be kept and turned over to the secretary for inclusion in the records of the association.

Non-Officer Members

Some bylaws place more stringent requirements on whom may be an officer but allow wider representation for the at-large membership of the board. Thus it may be permissible for renters, or even complete outsiders, to be elected to the board. Regardless, the remaining members of the board share equal voting rights with the officers of the corporation, but they do not have a specific role or title assigned to them.

Non-officer board members should expect to be somewhat less involved in the day-to-day minutiae of overseeing the association. However, all board members should be kept broadly informed of changes in the status of projects or any significant and unusual issues that may arise between meetings. Non-officers should receive status reports from the property manager, as well as any other documentation necessary to prepare for the regular board meetings. Any member may also be asked to act as board liaison to a homeowner committee or to assist with a special project.

When to Resign

Other than for specific personal reasons, there are two situations when it is best for a board member to resign: overwork and boredom.

Overworked generally applies to the president, who will see far more e-mails, take more phone calls and meet more people than any other board member. But it can also apply when board members have worked through difficult times or overseen large, involved projects. As burnout sets in, attention to details slip and the general performance of the board will decrease. No board member should be embarrassed to stand up and say "I need a break!" Leaving the board today does not mean a later return is out of the question. In fact, a second stint on the board a few years later may prove far more productive as the learning curve is over.

Boredom is the bane not just of board members, but of their fellow residents too, as boredom *costs money*. Any board member who begins to look for things to do on the property because there is nothing else to do on the horizon or worse, just because reserves have accumulated, should step down. The job of the board is *not to create work*, but to manage and maintain the existing property. Unless there is a very specific need which has been articulated by a significant number of homeowners, do not go off looking for projects. Do not spend reserves or place the association in debt in order to add a multi-million dollar wing to the clubhouse to hold an art gallery. Instead, enjoy this quiet time on the board, or step down and pursue additional activities available in one's own personal life.

Meetings

ALTHOUGH BYLAWS GENERALLY DO NOT MANDATE a board to hold any meetings other than the annual meeting of the share or unit holders, as a practical matter most will meet throughout the year. This chapter covers issues related to regular board meetings.

If the association does not have a common area facility that can be used for meetings, the board needs to establish where they will meet, either each month or in advance for the entire calendar year. Ideally, it should be a place with as few external distractions as possible. If a board member's home is used, the spouse and any children should not be present, both to avoid possible interruptions as well as to maintain the confidentiality of certain discussions. A bar or restaurant may be an acceptable choice if there is an area that can be used which is quiet and out of the way, but having the baseball game on a TV above the meeting table almost certainly will lead to items being skipped over and details missed. Caution should also be observed if meetings are in public to avoid confidential discussions in earshot of others. Just because no resident is seen nearby does not mean one of their friends or business associates is not!

Most mid- and larger-sized associations have an on-site clubhouse or similar building suitable to hold the board meeting.

If this facility is open to the residents, notice must be given to reserve the room or building for board use at the appointed date and time. A good rule to have is that meetings should always start promptly at the appointed time. To do so, board members must arrive at least five or ten minutes before the start of the meeting. Doing so allows a few minutes to dispense with the usual chit-chat among other members, as well as residents if the meeting is an open session. The property manager will typically want to distribute paper work to the board and may need a signature from an officer on a document. This too is best dispensed with prior to the official start of the meeting. Remember that an open meeting may also require the property manager or board members to put out several chairs for the residents in attendance.

When and How Often

The board is obliged to follow any meeting schedule set out in the bylaws, but many will give the board wide latitude in setting dates and times most convenient to those who must attend. Any development more than a few years old probably has in place some schedule which has been used in the past. This is a good starting point, but do not be afraid to alter it down the road. For instance, a mid- to larger-sized development likely requires a monthly board meeting, but it may have started out on a quarterly schedule when new as then there were few issues to handle over the course of a year. Perhaps the board is now meeting monthly but finds there are certain times of year when not much is on the agenda. In this case, holding regular meetings except for those months would be appropriate.

There is always great temptation to skip one of the summer months simply because it is summer, and people would prefer to do other things. That is a poor excuse as most meetings are held on a weeknight. It is also fraught with peril; the time most work is done at an association is the April to October period, with June through September the busiest months (In very hot climates, more work may be done in the winter months while the peak summer months are quieter.) December is another tempting month to skip – it is the holiday season, right? However, annual budgets are usually approved at that time of year, and any last minute preparations for winter must be evaluated and approved. Only skip a December meeting if all loose ends for the year have been taken care of by the close of the November meeting.

Probably the best months to consider skipping a formal meeting are November, January and February. For many, February may be the ideal month to skip as schools often have a Presidents Day holiday and board members with children will want time off to be with them. Likewise, those with the means may view February as the peak month for ski and island travel. So, short of a calamity, pencil in February as a month off!

In consultation with the property manager, the board also needs to select a particular day of the month for its meetings that all can agree on, e.g., the third Wednesday of the month. There will be times when this date must be changed due to work obligations, travel, etc., but the board should do its best to stick to it. Note that the board will not want to schedule meetings for the first or second week of the month unless the management agency is certain it can provide the financial and other statements from the prior month (or quarter, if that is the schedule). After that, choose a time – 7:00 or 7:30 P.M. seem to be common and will fit most board members' work schedules and also be agreeable to the property manager. Dinner can be a challenge on meeting nights, especially for board members who commute or travel long distances to their jobs. Even so, try not to make a habit of board members bringing dinner to the meeting.

The duration of the meetings can vary greatly depending on exactly what has been happening on the property and what upcoming work or projects are scheduled. Another factor is whether the association holds open or closed board meetings.

For a very sleepy property, an hour is probably enough. Larger properties, and those which may have special needs, can expect meetings to last from 90 minutes to three hours. The key is to be organized and on point in all discussions. The property manager is positioned to act as both a moderator and referee, as necessary, to keep the meeting focused and the comments and questions pertinent to the current agenda item. A long meeting is not a bad thing, so long as the board covers its agenda items and the necessary decisions are made. A long meeting with few accomplishments is just a waste of everyone's time.

Ultimately, longer meetings today should lead to shorter meetings in the future as problems in the association are solved and projects completed. This is especially true when the property has been mismanaged or neglected by prior boards and management agencies; the current board will have many issues to handle before the association is back on the right track.

Open or Closed

An important decision for any new board to make is whether their meetings will be public (open) or private (closed). It is a good idea to be consistent, and make the meeting type and procedures a matter of policy to avoid any confusion for the homeowners and residents.

The prospect of holding open meetings may be terrifying to some, or even all, of the board members. "We'll never get anything done!" "They'll just yell at us and ask stupid questions!" will be typical of the concerns voiced by board members, and they are legitimate concerns when open meetings are not structured and run properly.

First and foremost, open board meetings are not homeowner meetings held on a more frequent basis. They are simply working meetings of the directors that homeowners and residents may attend, and under certain circumstances, ask questions or offer their opinions. The primary goal is to complete the board's work. The secondary goal is to have an informed community.

There are many advantages of an informed community. The annual meeting will be faster and smoother as most questions and issues will have been addressed by the board over the course of the year. Backed up with an occasional community-wide letter or a periodic newsletter, there will be few homeowners who feel the need to ask "What has the board been up to?" This helps the board to put the annual meeting on its terms by limiting the Q&A to new business, eliminating the typical bickering over why this or that was or was not done.

An informed association is also of advantage, to both the board and management agency, in the day-to-day operation of the community. Homeowners who have a reasonable knowledge of the board's plans and when work is scheduled are far less likely to pester board members or the property manager with questions about work plans and project time lines.

Finally, rumor, innuendo and speculations of secret dealings are all but eliminated. When finances, policy and contracts are openly debated for any homeowner to hear, it is difficult to accuse the board of having a hidden agenda or other secrets. No board is perfect; all will have missteps, some small, some large. Being able to discuss problems openly will also avoid the inevitable claims of cover-ups or other misdeeds.

The downside of open meetings are that they require more discipline by the board. It is very easy to give in to the raised hand in the back of the room, and that may lead to time spent on tangential issues not critical to the point at hand. Therefore, there must be a policy in place specifying how the meeting is to be run and when homeowner comments and questions will be accepted (if at all). For most, holding the questions until the end of the open session will be the best way for the board to streamline the meeting. The president may need to adjust the time allotted for this Q&A based upon attendance and if the agenda item(s) are controversial. A good starting point is to allot 15 minutes to the homeowners.

After switching from private to public meetings, the first few meetings are often well attended, and the board is best off showing some flexibility by allowing all who wish to speak the opportunity. In that situation, before opening the floor, state that due to the large number of homeowners with questions there will be a limit of one question per person. As time goes by, the average attendance at the regular board meetings should drop to a small core group who are interested or simply have nothing better to do that night. Do not discount their value; most will inevitably discuss something about the meeting with one of their neighbors or friends.

It is also a good idea for the secretary to maintain a sign-in sheet of the homeowners and residents who attend the meeting. This information can be included in the minutes along with any questions or comments they may make later during the Q&A.

However, from time to time, there may be an issue or project on the table for which it is appropriate to pause for comments or questions. In particular, if the majority of the non-board attendees are there for just that one agenda item, dispensing with their questions sooner, rather than later, is the correct call. Information is fresh in everyone's mind, and hopefully the board will not need to rehash points made only minutes before. This is also a courtesy to those present and can serve to build some good will. If the subject is one of some importance to the community, pausing to ask for brief comment can also be an excellent way to take the pulse of the association before the board makes a major decision or commitment. Do not be surprised if a point is raised that the board has missed entirely.

There will often, if not always, be one portion of the regular meeting which will be private by necessity. During this "executive session," the board may discuss homeowner versus homeowner complaints, homeowner arrears or other sensitive issues.

Procedures

Meeting procedures can vary widely depending on the number of board members, the amount of business to conduct and whether meetings are open or closed, to name but a few variables.

All meetings should begin prior to the actual event with the preparation of an agenda by the president, perhaps in conjunction with the property manager. Some items will be recurring, others will change from month to month. An example agenda is given in Figure 1. When complete, the agenda should be sent to the entire board for their review and possible additions. Once finalized, it should be redistributed, and if board meetings are open, posted publicly.

The meeting will be called to order at the appropriate time by the president. Try to start as close as possible to the planned time, even if this means one or two board members will miss the first few minutes (which typically have no new information or decision making). Just be sure to have the necessary quorum prior to starting so that the meeting is official. The president will then dispense with any formalities or other legalities required by the bylaws.

Next up is the approval of minutes from the prior meeting(s). The president should ask whether all board members have read the minutes and if changes or corrections are necessary. If a board member has not had time to read the minutes, *they should not vote to accept the minutes.* It is at the discretion of the president to allow additional, in-meeting time to read past minutes. This should not be done unless necessary. If an insufficient number of board members have read the minutes, a motion can be made to defer acceptance until the next meeting. This could happen if the secretary was unable to furnish the documents in a timely manner to the board. Likewise, if major changes or corrections need to be made, acceptance should also be deferred. Once the board is satisfied with the minutes, a

Figure 1 Example Meeting Agenda

THE PINES HOMEOWNERS ASSOCIATION

Board of Directors
Tentative Agenda

November 17, 2011 7 PM

Call to Order
Approval Resolutions and Minutes of Prior Meeting

Report of Managing Agent

Report of the President
Report of the Treasurer

Parking Lot Signage
Painting Project Update
Approval of 2012 Pool Contract
First Draft 2012 Operating Budget*

Status of Homeowner Committees
Old Business
New Business

Open Forum For Homeowners

Executive Session

The board welcomes homeowners to attend the open session of the directors meeting held in the Pines Annex. The board requests home owners who attend the meeting reserve their questions and comments until all agenda items have been addressed at which time the floor will be opened to the home owners for approximately 15 minutes..

Home owners and residents may send questions and comments to the board at ANY time by writing to pinesboard@thepineshoa.com or in care of our managing agent, Forrest Management via phone (888-1234) or mail (21 Chestnut Ave., Glades Park PA 13131 member should move to accept them with minor corrections, if necessary. At that point, it is up to the secretary to sign the original copy of the minutes and provide it to the management agency for the association's files. The minutes are also given to the auditor by the management agency.

Less frequently, the board may have other documents that should be approved and formally recorded at the same time as the meeting minutes. Examples include: board procedures, codes of conduct, and proclamations officially approving large contracts. This should be a simple formality, with the content and structure of the documents having been discussed at prior meetings or by e-mail between sessions. Once motioned and accepted, the original documents are provided to the management agency.

After the minutes and other miscellaneous paperwork are dispensed with, the officers can give a brief summary of what they have been working on since the previous meeting. Depending on the level of intra-meeting communication among board members, this may be a few quick remarks or something a little more detailed. It is also of benefit to any residents in attendance. If the remarks are taking much more than two or three minutes each, provide them in writing to the other board members prior to the meeting. The secretary will include those comments with the meeting minutes and copies can also be made available to any residents in attendance. Remember, this is only a brief summary and additional details will be discussed, if appropriate, later in the meeting. Typically, only the president and treasurer will have comments. The treasurer should read for the record the bank and loan balances of the association and summarize any work done on financial projects, such as the annual audit. The secretary may, from time to time, wish to include in the minutes that certain legal or record keeping matters have been completed.

Before tackling any specific agenda items, the property manager should give the agent report, which should defer points related to specific agenda items until later in the meeting. The board should do their best to allow the property manager to complete each section of this report before interrupting to ask questions. Doing so allows the meeting to go faster, as a good property manager will have already anticipated the board's questions and will answer them in the report. Much of the agent report is mundane – a light was fixed, the pool permit granted, etc., and can be moved through very quickly. There may be points, though, for which board input is required – should a notice be sent? When?

To be effective, the board needs to stay on topic and not open a new can of worms every time the property manager asks for input or a member has a question. If they are reminded of something which the agent may need to look into, board members should hold off until the report is complete; the property manager may already be aware and has just not yet covered it. If not, the item will be considered new business and other board members can then comment on it as well. Any major concerns should be noted and discussed later in the meeting in more depth or as an agenda item at the next meeting. This allows the current meeting to proceed as planned and helps reduce the tendency to operate in crisis mode.

The heart of the meeting revolves around specific agenda items that require more extensive discussion or review. The goal of the president and property manager should be to prioritize these items so as to keep the total meeting to an acceptable length. A reasonable starting target is a two hour meeting. This allows 30 minutes for the preliminary items above, an hour for agenda items, and 30 minutes more for the executive session and any miscellaneous items. The board should definitely try to cap any meeting at three hours. Meetings generally are shortest in the winter months, when little is going on, and longest in late spring and early summer, when projects are planned and work performed.

A rule of thumb is three solid agenda items and up to three

minor items per meeting. Examples of minor items are a wrap up review of a just completed project (payments have been made, the work site is restored, etc.), or the final review or approval of a proposal the property manager has been working on, perhaps a security camera system for the pool area. Major items are plans for a painting project or some other significant capital project. Because they are short and easy to stay on topic, get the minor items out of the way first. Once they are disposed of, everyone knows it is time to focus on the big items. If a minor item takes much more than five minutes, it must be tabled, discussed further by e-mail and then added as an agenda item for the next meeting.

Again, a heavy burden will fall on the property manager and president to direct the discussion through the major and minor points of each issue at hand. If the discussion is of a large project, only certain elements should be brought up at any one meeting so as not to overwhelm board members or bog down in "what abouts." Except for emergency agenda items, preliminary discussions on major items should have already taken place between the board members, by e-mail or phone. This allows the president to anticipate what types of questions or problems are likely in full discussion and reduces the chance of any board member being caught off guard at the meeting.

The property manager should be well prepared and provide board members with the appropriate documentation, photos, plans, contracts, letters, etc., as relates to these items. When practicable, e-mail should be used to provide the board with hard copy in advance of the meeting. Board members should never read a contract or review a report for the first time during the meeting as it is impossible to formulate pertinent questions and weigh competing interests in the short time available. To be effective, all material should be made available at least three days, if not a week, ahead of the scheduled meeting.

It is always best if one board member leads the discussion; most often this is the president. However, if the board designates a specific member or sub-committee for oversight of a project or task, that member or committee should become the principal, and the president must try to defer as is reasonably appropriate. It is important for the president to show respect to the other members and not steal their thunder or needlessly badger them with questions. However, the president still retains the ultimate authority to determine when to change the focus of or conclude a presentation or discussion.

If the board holds open meetings, general guidelines will have already been established as to when the residents may ask questions or make statements. It is at the board's (and primarily the president's) discretion to modify those guidelines and stop during the discussion of an agenda item to take, or perhaps solicit, input from the gallery. There are no hard and fast rules on when and how to handle this – the time given and questions allowed will depend a lot on the significance of the project, the number of residents in attendance, the number who seem eager to contribute their thoughts, etc. Do not hesitate to put a time limit on this Q&A at the onset and limit to one question and one speaker per home. The board can, if they feel it appropriate, extend the time allowed and take additional questions and statements. It is best to close the floor when repetition sets in or simply ask for a show of hands if concerns seem to have coalesced around a few points. In any event, the board must be respectful to those speaking from the floor and treat them the same as they would hope to be treated if not now sitting on the board. Besides the diversity of opinion, try to use the experiences of the residents to the board's advantage; a carpenter may alert the board to issues and concerns with which they might not otherwise be familiar.

Larger projects, particularly in the feasibility and planning stages, can be difficult for a board to discuss efficiently. There may be so many variables and questions that focus is lost and little firm ground is settled. The president (or other project leader) must cut these discussions short and instead request that board members submit in writing (e-mail) a list of questions or concerns by a specific date. These lists can go directly to the property manager or first to the president to be organized and perhaps streamlined. Once in hand, the property manager or possibly a subcommittee of the board will attempt to find reasonably complete answers to the questions and provide a summary to the entire board before the next meeting. This allows for a much better subsequent discussion, or at least the ability to more quickly move forward to the next set of issues.

Once the agenda items are finished, there is usually a brief discussion of old and new business, and reports from home-owner committees (if they exist). Old business are items which remain open but incomplete (e.g., inspection of patios, collection of fines). The board may move that one or more of these items should get higher priority by the property manager or the board at the next meeting. New business items occur when board members or the property manager raise issues not already before the board. These could be small items, such as recycling bins being left outside too long after pickup, or something larger, such as the observation that some of the fencing around the property is damaged and needs to be repaired or replaced.

Some associations provide for the establishment of committees by homeowners that are overseen by the board. Examples are social or pool committees. Unless there is a very specific issue or event of note, reporting is usually perfunctory and by the board member liaison to the committee.

At this point, the open session is concluded and the resident attendees are asked to leave. After a very brief break, the board reconvenes in executive session. This is when the board discusses matters which would not be appropriate for the general population to hear. Do not use this as a time to hide problem issues unless their widespread knowledge would restrict the actions available to the board. An example of a legitimate closed session issue is when a problem is found involving a contractor working on a project and the board needs to determine what course of action to pursue to fix or resolve the problem. As this could involve weighing the pros and cons of legal actions or settlement offers, the discussions are properly not public until an ultimate resolution is achieved. At that point, the board should determine the proper way to inform the community of its actions, e.g., by a formal notice or by the inclusion of a written summary, including the board's reasoning, at the next open session.

The primary item discussed in the executive session is arrearages and what to do about them. Almost all boards are advised to keep these discussions private as to do otherwise may reveal personal financial information that should be considered confidential. There may also be statutory legal restrictions that serve to restrict which types of information the board may reveal publicly and when they may do so. Arrears are discussed in more detail in the *Arrears* chapter.

The board may also feel it necessary to have their attorney present to discuss a particular association problem. With few exceptions, those discussions are held in private executive session. Another example is if the board wished to interview contractors prior to awarding a contract. Having residents present could be an unnecessary and potentially unwelcome distraction for the contractor or vendor. Scheduling of the session is always done to best accommodate the needs of the visitor, who will be attending after normal work hours.

The secretary of the association is responsible for keeping a separate set of minutes that are clearly marked "Executive Session, Confidential." These minutes can be approved with the regular session minutes but any requests for corrections should only be made during the executive session. If a request is made to the management agency for a copy of the board meeting minutes, the executive session minutes will not be provided to residents.

To summarize, the regular open board meeting is broken into five sections: introductory items, the property manager report, agenda items, closing items and executive session. A board which holds closed meetings would follow a similar structure, though executive session items of an open meeting will instead become property manager or agenda items of the closed meeting.

Homeowner Relations

HOW MEMBERS OF THE ASSOCIATION PERCEIVE the board can have a significant effect on its ability to smoothly manage the affairs of the association. The board does not operate in a vacuum; everything the board does or does not do will be scrutinized. Board members may not have realized when they joined the board that in addition to being a manager, they are de facto politicians. In many ways, a board member is like a congressman with the officers a kin to committee chairman. Their constituents are both those homeowners who elected them to the board as well as those who abstained or voted for another candidate, again not very different than a congressman. This is not to suggest that board members should be in perpetual re-election mode. Rather, it is critical for board members to understand that politics will be present among board members, as well as between the board and the homeowners and residents.

Interactions at Meetings

The board interacts with homeowners at the annual meeting, special meetings, open board meetings and during executive session of regular or special board meetings. Though some aspects will vary, the common thread for handling the homeowner conversation at each type of meeting is: *treat the homeowner with the same respect you would expect of a board member were it you asking the question or making a statement.*

This can be a challenge. The board needs to interact with a wide range of homeowners: young, old, healthy, sick, rich, poor, polite, rude, brief and long winded, those with problems and those with agendas, hidden or not. In every case, the goal should be to treat each person fairly, with respect and to have as much patience as possible to hear them out and make progress in resolving their concerns.

In handling the angry or rude homeowner, remember that *something* has motivated them to contact the board in person, requiring not just their time but also conformity with the board's schedule. The board should immediately try to get the conversation away from an angry shouting match and instead, to a more even headed exchange of facts and opinions. If necessary, explain to the homeowner that the board is there to hear their problem and to try to find a solution as quickly as possible. After the president or property manager has given the homeowner the go ahead to describe their problem, allow them to speak uninterrupted until done. Board members should note down any questions they have during this time. By following this approach, the homeowner is allowed to blow off some steam without feeling as if they are being interrogated. Once finished, the board can then begin to ask follow-up questions or seek clarifications. The property manager is also likely to be aware of the problem and can explain what has, or has not, been done from their side and the events which have led up to this meeting.

Under no circumstances should board members engage in a back and forth shouting match with the homeowner. In no way make this a personal issue or add fuel to the confrontation. This is especially important if the meeting is the annual meeting or an open monthly board meeting where other homeowners are present. Sinking to the level of the loud, rude or confrontational homeowner will hurt the image of the board and its members far more than that of the homeowner. Those in attendance might see that homeowner as rude, hostile or crazy; they are quite likely to apply those same adjectives to the board and add arrogant and insensitive to the list. In the event the board and property manager are unable to get the homeowner to discuss the matter civilly, the president or property manager will have to break the conversation and ask the homeowner to put their entire complaint in writing. Inform the homeowner that the board will review the complaint with the property manager and schedule a private meeting with them after that time.

The board must never forget that homeowner perception will affect their ability to manage the association smoothly. If the board or its officers are viewed as arrogant, insensitive or confrontational, they are likely to receive excessive scrutiny and pushback from the members of the association for even the smallest thing they attempt to do. This can lead to a vicious cycle where every rule change, maintenance issue or capital project leads to a firestorm of protest from affected homeowners, regardless of how necessary or reasonable the board's actions.

Instead, by taking the high ground and sometimes turning the other cheek in the face of belligerence, the board can establish itself as a fair minded body and one that is willing to listen to all the homeowners, take their feelings into account and act in a professional manner. As time goes by, the board will find that fewer homeowners question its decisions and more are willing to help make the community a better place to live. A large development may have homeowners who are police officers, lawyers, government officials or specialists in certain trades. They are far more likely to provide tips and other helpful information to the board voluntarily if the board is viewed in a positive light by the entire association.

Non-meeting Interactions

Do not think for a moment that a board member will only receive comments or questions during board meetings. That is just the idyllic dream of every board member in the world! The reality, however, is that homeowners and residents will see board members picking up mail, getting in or out of their cars, at the pool or even at the supermarket and deem that a perfect opportunity to ask (or yell) about some issue of concern to them.

If not too hurried, it can build good will if the board member in question takes a moment to hear the homeowner out and offer a brief comment, trying not to look put off if they do so. Unless the homeowner has brought something unique or of great concern, keep the conversation short, to the point and always end it by saying that "In the future you should contact the property manager, they can help you much faster than I can and I would feel terrible if I forgot to follow up with them on your problem. They keep a record of calls and e-mails to make sure nothing is missed and that allows the entire board to see what problems the residents are having. I'm going to leave them a message, but please make sure you follow up with them in a day or two as well." By handling the encounter this way, the board member has shown that they are concerned about the homeowner's problem but have also made clear they prefer to hear about it from the property manager, not the homeowner.

Of course, there will be situations when a board member simply does not have the time or it is otherwise inconvenient to speak to the homeowner. In that case, they should politely state there is some obligations they must deal with immediately and suggest the homeowner e-mail their concern, copying the property manager. When they next see the homeowner, the board member can say they have read the homeowner's e-mail and that the property manager or the board will be following up as necessary. If it is an elderly, off-line homeowner, bite the bullet and either suggest a time to speak with them or offer to return their phone call the next day.

However, it is quite possible to minimize these types of encounters if the board is proactive in keeping the homeowners and residents informed of the goings-on in the community by the posting of notices or distribution of a periodic newsletter.

Newsletter

Perhaps oddly, doing a good job may lead to unintended problems if homeowners are caught by surprise when significant changes are afoot. The number of homeowners who are interested in attending annual or open monthly board meetings is inversely proportional to how well the property is being managed. If the board is doing a good job, they may need to use additional methods to keep the homeowners and residents informed about important decisions or events.

One way is to publish a short newsletter each quarter that gives a brief recap of any significant items from the monthly board meetings or of work completed on the property during the quarter. Any important plans or topics the board expects to address in the near future should also be mentioned. The newsletter can also include preliminary drafts of the annual budget, significant rule changes, photos from social events and reminders about parking, pet or other policies. Content can be provided as necessary by the various officers, regular board members and residents.

The property manager probably will not wish to prepare the newsletter unless it is required under the management contract, so a board member(s) or resident will need to take charge. The presentation does not need to be particularly fancy to communicate the essentials – a simple letter format will work and is in the grasp of anyone with even minimal computer expertise (Use both sides of the paper when printing or copying for distribution.) Multi-column formats, or those including photos, are only slightly more complex and should be familiar territory for many office workers. The board may wish to establish a "communications" homeowner committee to help prepare and distribute the newsletter and other documents, such as a residents manual or a welcome kit for new homeowners and residents.

A periodic newsletter has one tremendous side benefit: it will greatly shorten the length of the annual meeting. There will be no need for an extensive rehash of the board's work of the prior year, nor its near term plans, as the homeowners are already well informed. A quick, cursory review that hits on the big points is all that will be necessary before focusing on any significant new plans. The number of questions asked by homeowners will be greatly reduced and targeted at the future plans, not the past events. With luck, the roll call of homeowners and election of new directors will take up most of the meeting.

The board may also be tempted to move all communications with the homeowners to the many electronic options available today. However, hard copy has the advantage of being accessible to older members of the association; to the shock and horror of younger board members, many older residents may still be "off-line." The opt-in nature of electronic media is also a disadvantage over the impossible to ignore presence of a paper newsletter stuck in a door or mailbox. That said, electronic communication is an increasingly important way to stay in touch with the membership of the association and will be covered in greater detail in *Appendix D.*

Residents Manual

Most HOAs maintain a list of rules and regulations passed by the board or stated explicitly in the bylaws and homeowners' agreement. Unfortunately, this documentation is frequently poorly worded, incomplete and badly formatted – often just a series of photocopied pages with a staple in the top corner.

Pages are easily lost and sooner than later, the remainder is tossed in the trash or put with the documentation for the home appliances, never to be seen again.

With little additional time and effort, the board, perhaps in conjunction with a homeowner communications committee, can prepare an attractive document that is far less likely to be put in the garbage and is more likely to be consulted when a homeowner needs a quick answer about a specific rule or phone number. With the advent of extremely low cost self-publishing solutions from companies, such as Amazon.com and Lulu.com, there is no excuse to be using the office supply store to run off photocopies. With judicious timing and the use of publisher and volume discounts, a 25 to 30 page residents manual can be purchased for about $3.50 a copy. All that is required is a nicely formatted document and a photo of your community for the front and back covers. Most of the self-publishing firms provide on-line "wizards" and templates that will guide the author step by step through the process, offering feedback and suggesting corrections that need to be made before the document is press ready. A board or committee member already able to create a document on their computer is 90% of the way to a final product.

The residents manual should offer a concise explanation of how the association operates and what is expected of the homeowners and residents. If the board has adopted formal policies, these too should be included (e.g. an arrears policy) An example table of contents is shown in Figure 2.

When writing the residents manual, the author(s) will need to strike a balance between providing sufficient information to answer the most common questions in reasonable depth and providing something which attempts to answer every "but what about ...?" One way to handle the task of writing the manual is to divvy up a section to each board member, thus reducing the work load on any one member. The downside is that the tone of each section will be different, but since most homeowners do not read the manual cover to cover, this should not be a major

Figure 2 Example table of contents

1. The Homeowners Association
   - 1.1 Management of The Pines
     - Bylaws and Homeowners' Agreement
     - Rules and Regulations
     - Annual Meeting
     - Website
     - Additional Information
     - Committees
   - 1.2 Common Charges
   - 1.3 Guests and Residents
2. Grounds
   - 2.1 Garbage Collection and Recycling
   - 2.2 Landscaping
   - 2.3 Pest Control
   - 2.4 Snow Removal
3. Common Areas
   - 3.1 Clubhouse: Use and Rental
   - 3.2 Swimming Pool
   - 3.3 Tennis Courts
   - 3.4 Parking
4. Exterior Alteration of Homes
5. Miscellaneous
   - 5.1 Insurance Requirements
   - 5.2 Management Agent
6. Appendix
   - A Arrears Policy
   - B Garbage Policy
   - C Pet Policy
   - D Clubhouse and Pool Rental Agreement

concern. When finished, a draft copy should be circulated to all board members to catch omissions or inconsistencies. Copy editing and formatting can be left until the final draft to avoid becoming bogged down in process at the expense of content. When complete, the board should officially approve the manual at a regular monthly board meeting, establish how many copies will be ordered and task the property manager with arranging for the distribution to all residents and absentee homeowners.

Homeowner on Homeowner

The board and property manager must sometimes resolve complaints which are between homeowners. Many are for rule infractions (parking, pets) but complaints can also relate to personal behaviour (too loud, intimidating). The old adage that "there are three sides to every story: his, hers and the truth" really does come into play when dealing with these situations.

The easiest to handle are when a homeowner from one area files a complaint for a rules infraction against a homeowner from another part of the complex, perhaps for speeding or not observing traffic signs. The situation becomes more difficult, however, when the complaints are from neighbors or close by units. Do not underestimate the ability of homeowners to be petty, vindictive and to spy upon one another.

Assuming the complaint is either a rule or policy infraction, there are a few ground rules the board should follow in trying to resolve what could be a long running grievance. First, the property manager should be directed to contact both parties involved in the complaint, requesting clarifications as necessary from the complainant and the other side of the story from the subject of the complaint. The subject of the complaint should be advised it is in their best interest to follow-up in writing to the management agency to ensure their side of the story is accurately recorded. The property manager should then review the pertinent rules and regulations and decide whether a warning or fine is appropriate and notify the defendant of the decision and a specific time frame for any appeal. Depending on the nature of the complaint, the property manager may defer requesting the defendant's statement until this letter is sent. If subsequent communications cast doubt on the veracity of the original complaint, the property manager can modify or cancel the fine or warning. When the matter is settled, a letter or e-mail should go to the complainant stating that the matter has been resolved to the satisfaction of the board and management agency. Failure to do this may result in additional inquiries about the status of the complaint.

In the event of an appeal, or in a case where the property manager is unable to separate fact from innuendo, the entire matter should be forwarded to the board for review in conjunction with the property manager. Both parties should be notified that the matter will be before the board and be given an opportunity to speak directly to the board or enter further statements about the matter into the written record.

The board must act as an impartial body, and any members with a personal or other conflict with either of the parties should be recused from the review. In effect, the board acts as an appellate court and affirms or denies the ruling of the property manager. The board may also adjust the ruling or send it back to the property manager for additional review and research. In reviewing the case, the board needs to weigh not just the evidence but also the severity of the infraction, the reasonableness of the complaint and whether the bylaws even permit a ruling on the matter at hand.

The most difficult cases are those which affect quality of life and the enjoyment of the homeowner's property. Some bylaws will give the board discretion in dealing with such issues, but tread carefully. Beware of setting precedents allowing every triviality to be blown up to a major offense requiring the board to chose one side or another. The board, as a group, must decide if the original complaint is reasonable and further, if the defendant has been asked to take certain steps to alleviate the problem (or has done so voluntarily), were those also reasonable and sufficient to address the complainant's concerns.

There are some types of complaints the board should or must decline to be involved with. A complaint that a neighbor is too loud going up or down their inside stairs or that they play their television too loud or too late at night should be avoided. This type of complaint is very subjective, and unless the entire board were to be in the house when the "infraction" occurs, there is no way for the board to determine if in fact the neighbor's behavior was so egregious as to materially affect the complainant. And a letter sent, even if worded gently, to the subject of the complaint asking them to be more quiet inside their home may only inflame the situation, especially if the defendant had been on good terms (in their mind) with their neighbor. Most municipalities have noise ordinances, and the property manager can direct the complaining homeowner to file a police report if they feel the noise is excessive or at an improper hour. Even though the end result may still be tense relations between the two neighbors, the complainant will know very quickly whether there really is merit to their complaint or if the police simply walk away with no further action.

When the circumstances are clear, the board can act, though with care. A noise complaint against a homeowner who has a holiday barbeque on their patio probably does not rise to the level of a board reprimand. A noise complaint against a home-owner who has a barbeque every weekend from May through September with very loud music may require review and repri-mand. But remember, the qualifier should be *unreasonably* loud music and **not** that the homeowner simply plays music while having guests out of doors during the summer season, a fully legitimate use of their home and property.

Police

The board should *never* involve itself in matters which are outside of the scope of the homeowners' agreement or that do not occur on common property. Thus, if a homeowner lodges a complaint that they are being harassed by another homeowner, the property manager, and if necessary the board, should respectfully decline to act as it is outside the scope of the management of the property. For instance, were a homeowner to make unwanted romantic advances toward another, that is a matter for the police and not the association. Some board members may feel they have a "moral" obligation to act in some way, such as alerting others about the alleged advances, but this is wrong and can instead potentially lead to legal action against the association. Protecting individuals from one another is a job for the police, not the association. Members of the board must understand that their *primary* fiduciary obligation is to protect the association, in this example from a potential defamation of character civil litigation.

However, the board may take a stand against a homeowner or resident who is creating a "nuisance" *on the common property* that may, or may not, break local, state or federal laws. Again, because nuisance is open to interpretation, the board must be careful to apply a reasonableness test before taking any action.

If an incident involving an individual(s) occurs on common property, such as in the clubhouse or at the pool, the *board may only file a police report against them if the act in question is witnessed by a board member*. It is not sufficient for a homeowner to let the board know of the illegal or questionable behavior. In fact, the homeowner should have contacted the police on their own (and may still do so). Although the board may not infringe on the civil rights of any of its homeowners and residents, it may restrict access to common facilities and property based upon behaviour so long as the policy is already in place and applies equally to all residents. Always consult with the association's attorney when there may be doubt about what is common ground and to verify the applicable state laws and legal precedents. For example, unless the community is gated and access to the roads restricted, the roadways and parking lots may not be considered private property, common to association members, in the eyes of the court.

To avoid future lawsuits, even if frivolous, be certain that the rules and regulations and ramifications of failing to follow them are legally unambiguous. Ideally, the board wants a litigant's attorney to advise, without question, against filing suit against the association because there is no legal wiggle room to stand on and a monetary award is unlikely.

Rules And Regulations

Every HOA has a basic set of rules and regulations laid out in the bylaws and homeowners' agreement. In addition, the board is granted broad latitude to formulate additional rules and regulations as they deem necessary for the operation of the property.

Bylaws

The bylaws are the rules of the corporate entity that is the homeowners association; they are primarily focused on the corporate structure and generation of revenue. After defining the concept of membership in the association, there will be a detailed discussion of whom may vote at annual and special meetings of the association, how a vote may be cast and the various requirements that must be met to consider a meeting valid, such as having a quorum and giving proper and timely notice of the meeting. The secretary of the association must be familiar with the various notices that are required to be sent prior to the annual (or special) meeting as there may be specific language and timing constraints that must be observed. For instance, if the bylaws specify that notice be sent to homeowners no earlier than 30 days, but no less than ten days prior to the meeting, a failure by the secretary and property manager to do so can result in a legal challenge of any business that is transacted at that meeting, such as the election of directors or approval of financing or business plans.

Following next are procedures and definitions related to the board of directors (or managers), such as their number, term, powers and meeting requirements. How vacancies can be handled and removal of directors for cause are also addressed. Interestingly, not all bylaws restrict membership in the board of directors to just the members of the association; some permit renters or other occupants of the homes to be on the board. Vacancies on the board are most often filled by a vote of the directors rather than the membership due to the difficulty of assembling a quorum of the association's members. The powers of the board may be defined very precisely and extensively, or more often, with considerable room for interpretation. Always stated is the right to levy a common charge and special assessment on the membership, to hire a management agency, to hire contractors as needed to maintain the property and to make reasonable rules and regulations.

The officers of the board receive special mention to define how they are selected and their specific responsibilities. Again, there can be considerable variation in the method of electing officers as well as the specific requirements of eligibility. In some cases, officers are chosen by the board itself. In others, officers may be chosen based on the number of votes received in their election to the board. Some bylaws will allow non-members of the association to be officers, some will not require the officers to even be members of the board. The responsibilities of each officer are generally as set out in the earlier chapter on the structure of the board.

The bylaws will also give instructions on how how to amend or change the bylaws. Just as amending the Constitution of the United States is a difficult process, so to is amending the bylaws of an HOA. Often there is the need to have two-thirds of the *entire membership of the association* vote in favor of the changes at a special or annual meeting. As many associations struggle to achieve even a 50% quorum at the annual meeting, including proxies, this is indeed a high hurdle to change.

There will also be some discussion of assessments on the membership of the association, the transfer and sale of homes and the rights of the members of the association to inspect the books of the corporation.

Homeowners' Agreement

THE HOMEOWNERS' AGREEMENT, more formally known as the "declaration of covenants, restrictions, easements, changes and liens," is the document that sets out the responsibilities of the association, the homeowners and more generally what each may or may not do with regards to private property and the common areas. There may also be some overlap or repetition of topics, in whole or in part, between the homeowners' agreement and the bylaws, and the bylaws may reference specific sections of the homeowners' agreement.

Like the bylaws, the homeowners' agreement was written and filed with the appropriate government agency at the time the property was developed. As such, it will often contain a substantial amount of descriptive information about the property as a whole and language related to the granting of easements and rights-of-way to the developer and utility companies.

The creation of a lien and personal obligation with the conveyance of the deed of any property within the association will be described at length. This gives the parameters of how the monthly and other assessments can be made, their purpose, due dates and affects of non-payment.

Of interest to many homeowners are the sections concerning architectural control and party walls and fences. Architectural control is catch-all for "The board must approve any changes to the homes and possibly the landscaping around it as well." In order to give the homeowner some protection, there can be a requirement that the board act upon any requests to make alterations within a specific time frame, such as 60 days after receipt. If the board does not act in that time frame, the homeowner's request is to be considered approved or that approval is not required and their plans may proceed. The board will rarely, if ever, have any involvement in issues related to the ownership and repairs to party walls and fences as these are viewed as resources shared between two homeowners. The board should decline involvement in these types of disputes, and remind both parties to consult the homeowners' agreement for further information. The board may, however, place conditions on the materials used in any repairs or replacement involving the exteriors of the home.

The board should carefully review any language concerning exterior maintenance. Besides the maintenance of common areas, there is usually a laundry list of items that are located on deeded property for which the association is required to assume responsibility. Depending on the types of buildings on the property, this can include the painting of the homes, repair and replacement of the roof, landscaping services on private properties, snow removal from private walks and the wires, pipes and conduits located outside the home which connect with the various utility and drainage systems. There is likely to be a section regarding the disrepair of lots that allows the board to request the homeowner effect repairs or maintenance to their property and uphold the general good appearance of the association. If the homeowner fails to do so, the board may perform the work and back bill the homeowner. For example, if the association is required to paint the siding of the homes, rotted or otherwise damaged wood needs to be replaced first, at homeowner expense.

The board must have a good understanding of what the

association is obligated to handle and what it is not. When in doubt, ask the association's attorney to clarify and interpret the language in a formal document for the board and management agency. In addition to satisfying fiduciary responsibilities, the ability to present such a document to any affected homeowner may reduce the chance of a lawsuit against the association for acting or failing to act within the legal obligations of the homeowners' agreement.

One item certain to cause problems is if the association is responsible for "the roof." What constitutes the roof? Is it shingles only? Shingles and tar paper? What about the plywood decking to which the shingles and tar paper are attached? Is flashing part of the roof? Clearly, the financial obligations to the association can vary greatly depending on how those questions are answered. In general, ambiguity of responsibilities is not uncommon and can cause frequent aggravation to the board.

The last substantial section in the homeowners' agreement, which concerns the use of the property by members and residents of the association, gives what are in effect starter rules and regulations as established at the inception of the development. However, unlike rules and regulations authored and passed by the board of directors, these rules and regulations may not be changed except by extraordinary measures, typically requiring $66\frac{2}{3}\%$ of the members of the association to sign off on any proposed amendments. And like the bylaws of the corporation, the homeowners' agreement is valid for a set period of time and automatically renews itself unless the association replaces it with a new instrument (in whole or part) signed by a very large majority of the members of the association – 80% in some cases, with equally stringent requirements on the replacement process.

Most of the rules speak to issues of appearance, parking, pets, nuisances and advertising or signage. Some rules, such as "dogs must be leashed at all times" are complete and easy to understand. Others, such as "no nuisances shall be allowed on the property" may be vague and subject to liberal interpretation. It is the latter that the board must be most concerned, and they should strive to establish more precise and complete definitions. For instance, the board may approve a short list of obvious nuisances with the understanding that it reserves the right to add to or modify the list at any time in the future. What the board may not do is to take away rights. If the homeowners' agreement grants each unit owner two designated parking spaces, the board may not reduce this to one space except by the passage of an amendment in accordance with the specific and legally binding procedures stated in the document.

Rules from the Board

AT ANY TIME THE BOARD MAY ESTABLISH additional rules which govern the use of the property, the actions of homeowners and regulate the board itself. All such rules and regulations should be formally adopted by the board, distributed to the members of the associations and when appropriate, to non-member residents. The management agency should keep copies on file to ensure that future boards are aware of the actions of their predecessors.

Regulating the Board of Directors

With power comes accusations of the abuse of that power and board members should realize there will be times when they are accused of bias, infidelity and irresponsible behavior. This is more likely to happen if the board has net yet taken action to codify a set of protocols that set forth ethical and operational rules which each member must sign and agree to follow. Four specific protocols are recommended: conflict of interest, code of conduct, emergency action and contracts policy.

Conflict of Interest

The conflict of interest policy (see the example in *Appendix A*) should establish that personal enrichment of board members, their families or business associates is not permitted. Members of the association do not wish to hear that the irrigation contract has been awarded to the brother-in-law of one of the board members, regardless of competency. Nor do they wish to know that the spouse of another member will be the new auditor. Contracts that may benefit a board member, directly or indirectly, in any professional capacity should not be awarded.

Perhaps those examples seem obvious, but that has not stopped many a board member across the country from taking advantage of their position. And the longer board members serve, the greater the temptation. This is *not* to say that every such case is one where financial gain was the primary intent. Inertia and complacency can provide just as much motivation for taking what may seem to be the easy way out. With the codification of rules to prevent conflict of interest, board members can be held to account by one other, the property manager and the members of the association.

Code of Conduct

A code of conduct policy does not need to be lengthy but should hit on several key points. Board members must not exhibit bias against another homeowner and if they feel they are unable to do so, they must recuse themselves from the matter before the board. Board members must not put certain members or groups of members of the association before others. Board members should always answer members honestly or defer answering until such a time as they are able to do so with candor. Board members should not ask the association's contractors or service providers for consideration above that given to the other members of the association. Members of the board are the direct representatives of the association and they should always act in a professional manner in dealings on behalf of the association with other firms and their employees.

Again, on paper these may seem to be obvious statements. In practice, however, they may not be followed. By requiring each board member to sign off on a code of conduct, the rest of the board, as well as the members of the association, are more easily able to reign in or dismiss a discourteous or unprofessional director.

Emergencies

It is important that every board have a formal emergency action policy. Board members travel for work and pleasure, may sometimes be hospitalized or otherwise unable to be on the property to see first hand or discuss a significant event. This could be a fire, storm damage, sewage line break or a death or serious injury on the common facilities or property. Even though the bylaws may specifically state that the vice president is authorized to perform the duties of the president if they are absent or unable to act, it is a good idea to have further backup, as well as a general idea of what constitutes an emergency that allows for this assumption of power. The treasurer is the ideal third in line due to their level of involvement in the day-to-day affairs of the association. The secretary, also being an officer, would round out the top four to take charge and interact with the property manager and other employees of the management agency during an emergency. Absent any of the officers, succession will have to fall to the non-officer members of the board, either by seniority or by some other means of the board's choosing.

Finally, if *no* member of the board is available and the property manager believes action absolutely *must* be taken, the board should provide the necessary authorization to do so. That authorization should be for a specific period of time, after which attempts again must be made to contact the various board members in succession order. The board must also authorize specific emergency spending powers and limits to each officer, alone or in combination, as well as to the property manager. Once a quorum of board members are available, additional funds can be approved if necessary. The board should consult with the property manager to determine what limits are customary and practical for the association's size. In conjunction with the emergency spending powers, the board can also define normal monthly discretionary spending limits for each officer and the property manager.

Having the above emergency policy in place will avoid needless waste of time and questions, just when the association can least afford a delay by either the board or the property manager. Make sure the board adopts one as soon as possible.

Contract Policy

The board should also have in place a protocol that describes what steps are required before approval can be granted for a contract or service agreement. A three or four tiered grouping by the amounts of money involved works well for most homeowner associations.

The first level is for small outlays, on the order of a few thousand dollars, when it is usually impractical to requests bids or quotes from many vendors. For that reason, the board may choose to have the property manager get one or two quotes from vendors they know and trust, or some other criteria set by the board (perhaps based on locality).

The next tier is for those jobs that are not small, are a fair sized outlay of funds but are not of the size to have a materially adverse affect on the association's finances or require extensive documentation, engineering or time to complete. The property manager should be required to locate three or four bidders and to send to them a request for quote that describes the material or service desired. References should be requested and the property manager or board required to verify each.

Insurance commensurate with the work being performed should be demanded. All terms of the quotes or contracts should be the same and the materials to be used specified in clear language. The association's attorney should be required to review the contract prior to final board approval. Here, the board must balance the need to be fiducially responsible in awarding the contract against the practical realities that most jobs this size are done by small companies and proprietorships who are not prepared or willing to handle an extensive or complex RFP (request for proposal). A reasonable cap on this tier is in the range of $50,000 to $100,000. If the work will modify structures, a requirement for engineering oversight might be included in certain situations.

The top tier is for the truly large jobs – painting projects, new roofs, repaving roads, etc. The proposal requests and contracts are more extensive than the lower tiers and can often be large legal documents, such as a standardized AIA (American Institute of Architects) roofing contract. The property manager can write the RFP with input from the board and review by the association's attorney before it is sent to prospective bidders. Specifications may be quite extensive, and often preliminary engineering work may be required. In these cases, the engineering firm may be the primary author of the RFP with the property manager, attorney and board suggesting additional, non-technical language they deem appropriate. The policy should also require that the board interview prospective bidders prior to sending out the RFP package.

Financing for large projects, if required, may be in an amount that the board feels it appropriate and necessary to receive the prior approval of the association's membership at a special meeting. Unless such a requirement is stated in the bylaws or homeowners' agreement, the terms of approval can be set by the board, i.e. a majority vote of those attending a special meeting. By requiring this type of consideration in the contract policy, the association protects its members from a board which has become consumed with the desire to "do something" but has lost touch with the abilities of its members to pay for the work. It is far better to know up front that the members are unwilling to assume a large debt or that enough are struggling financially in a poor economy to call into question their ability to pay a special assessment. The only recourse the board has available to respond to non-payment is foreclosure, which is a very slow and costly process. If enough members fail to pay a special assessment to repay the financing, the association may find they are faced with defaulting on a large loan or cutting out significant services, such as landscaping, in order to meet the required loan payments. For this reason, the board should also include a requirement that any loan payment not be in excess of a certain percentage of the regular common charge income of the association, say 25%.

Regulating the Residents

WHEN IT COMES TO RESIDENTS, the board has two considerations: what to regulate and how to enforce those rules. But regardless of those choices, the board must take care that the rules and regulations of the association are distributed to all homeowners. A simple photocopy may serve to meet the legal requirements per the bylaws and homeowners' agreement, but a better method is to incorporate all rules and regulations from the homeowners' agreement, bylaws and the board into one residents manual. This manual can also include other information, such as how to contact the management agency, when and where regular board meetings are held, how to rent the clubhouse, etc. Unlike one page photocopies, which can find their way into the trash very quickly, a residents manual is likely to be kept and referred to in the future.

An established community probably already has all the rules it requires, though a new association may not have codified anything beyond what is included in the homeowners' agreement. The latter should attempt to put in place a reasonable set of rules to cover most circumstances as soon as possible to avoid having to create them one by one as problems arise on the property. The former should review the established rules and regulations every three to five years to verify that none are obsolete, they are still functionally applicable and the wording is clear.

If the association is not yet using a residents manual, a good time to start would be after a formal review of the existing rules or the codification of an initial set of rules.

What to Regulate

It is often said that the powers of an HOA board are nearly limitless and although a bit of an exaggeration, there is great truth to the statement. That does not mean, however, that the board should take advantage of that power to establish a byzantine set of rules and regulations that attempt to provide for any possible action or occurrence on the property. Regulation fatigue is real, and at a certain point many residents will ignore or openly mock attempts at further regulation.

Only establish rules and regulations when absolutely necessary to the smooth and legal operation of the association. Parking, traffic flow and pool regulations are all reasonable and necessary. Trying to regulate the color of patio furniture is not. It is often assumed, wrongly, that "If it happens once it will happen all the time." A homeowner complains that a resident police officer has installed a front light with a bulb that is a greenish white (often used to identify police stations). They fear that if it is not changed to "white," there will be a plethora of oddly colored light bulbs at the entrance to each home. Of course, incandescent bulbs look different if the wattage is not the same, compact fluorescent are varied in appearance and certainly appear different than incandescents, and so on. In this example conformity is relative. The police officer's bulb is not so different from others to be objectionable and is unlikely to lead to the installation of truly objectionable bulbs by others. There is no need to consider a conformity regulation until such a time as there really is a problem – the slippery slope is greatly exaggerated.

Conformity type regulations, as would be required to placate the complaining homeowner, are difficult and time consuming to formulate and can prove to be very polarizing. In the above example, what constitutes a white light bulb? Short of specifying a specific brand, model and wattage it is impossible to achieve absolute conformity. Even were only one bulb allowed, what happens if it is suddenly discontinued? Must every homeowner then replace their existing bulbs with some other, newly approved model? The board should think long and hard before making additional conformity regulations and must always leave some degree of latitude to future proof the new rule.

Parking is one thing which is universally regulated, but is fairly simple to do if the focus is on the misuse of assigned spots: the use and duration of use of guest, handicapped and other spots with special designations; the storage of vehicles; and the parking of commercial vehicles. One issue often encountered in older developments is that guest spots are used on a regular basis by homeowners to park a second or third car. However, this issue may or may not be a significant problem. At the time the development was built, parking decisions may have been based on one car families as multi-car families in planned urban communities were rare. If the board determines that multi-car families are severely restricting the availability of guest parking for actual guests, action may be required to relocate the second and third vehicles to public street parking. But if there is still adequate parking available when needed, the board may be better off deferring additional regulation to the future. Another option is to limit the amount of time, say to 24 hours, that a guest spot may be used by a homeowner before the car must be moved in order to give others an equal opportunity to use that spot. The board also needs to consult the homeowners' agreement to determine if it defines who may use guest spots. If it includes homeowners, the best the board can do is limit the use to a reasonable amount of time as exclusion would be a violation of the homeowners' agreement.

The primary role of traffic regulations is the safety of pedestrians and other drivers, as well as ensuring the ability of emergency vehicles to enter and operate upon the property. That said, the board can only do so much – it can paint markings on the pavement until there is little blacktop left, but that will not guarantee compliance by the residents. Redundant markings will only mar the aesthetics of the development. One specific marking that is over used is "no parking." Only use this in areas where parking will truly obstruct other vehicles, and if it is for emergency vehicles, color and mark it as such. No parking markings placed where there is no obvious reason not to park will be ignored and create a battle the board and property manager really need not waste time fighting. The board will also need to decide on a case by case basis whether to use pavement markings or signs. For instance, small one way signs may delineate flow around a traffic circle while pavement markings may indicate split flow around an island or other features in the roadways.

Other regulations may already be mandated by municipal authorities and present a liability risk to the association if the board does not comply with specific notification and enforcement requirements. The most common example relates to the operation a pool on common property – Board of Health mandated safety rules must be displayed prominently along with any other signage they may require.

How to Enforce

The rules and regulations are in place, now how to enforce them? To start, the board should have a uniform fine system for violations of the parking, traffic, pet and other policies. Warnings and subsequent offenses must carry specific dollar fines and the durations that each will stay on the books before rolling off. Some infractions, such as violation of mandatory pool regulations or failure to follow the direction of the lifeguard, should result in the loss of those privileges for a specified period of time in addition to a mandatory fine.

With the penalty structure in place, the board now must ask *who will enforce the rules?* Should board members note down every infraction they see and have the property manager log the information? The board needs to think long and hard before going down that route. Though possible, it is *not* advisable for the board to be the police of the association.

Maintaining cordial relations with neighbors is challenging enough for most board members when disagreements arise over the actions the board has taken. Adding in fines and other penalties, based only on board member observations, is a sure fire way to generate significant resentment and isolate the board members. Homeowners are likely to feel they are being spied upon by the board and may believe they are guilty until proven innocent. Two way information flow between the board and homeowners is likely to decline as well. The board must ask if they are fostering an environment where the residents enjoy living or one where they must constantly look over their shoulder in fear?

Except for safety type infractions, a better way is to allow the residents to police one other. The board does not need to chase down every parking infraction if no one is actually complaining about parking problems. Homeowners will generally tolerate the occasional policy infraction by their neighbors as they know that they. too, will suffer a misstep from time to time. Perhaps a resident has done some spring cleaning on a Sunday afternoon and has put out a number of trash bags. The pick-up is not until Tuesday. Technically, the homeowner may be in violation of the garbage policy, which says nothing is to be put out until the night before the pick-up. Does the board member who notices this need to fire off an e-mail to the property manager to fine that homeowner? Arguably not, as it is a one-off rare event. Now, if the same resident did this every week, it is quite likely the property manager already has had complaints from residents living nearby and should take the appropriate actions per the policy.

The board is best off to put itself in the position of being an appeals court. The residents are the police; the property manager is the investigative judge who will gather facts and recommend the appropriate fine or action to take against the offending resident. Should the offender disagree with the allegation or the fine, the board is in a position where they can fairly review the facts, extenuating circumstances and any actions already taken. The board should not be the judge, jury and executioner.

Issues of safety, however, do require the board to act when they see a violation. The board, for liability reasons, cannot allow those types of infractions to pass by. Driving on the wrong side of the street, cutting the top of a traffic circle, going very fast or diving in a no diving area are all serious infractions which could lead to harm to person or property.

When complaints are made, whether by homeowners, the property manager or the board, all efforts should be made to record as much identifying information as possible. This includes the date and time, the person involved, the infraction type and if it involves a vehicle, the make, model and plate number. In addition to defining the rules, regulations and penalties, the residents manual should also include a paragraph describing the information necessary to file a proper complaint, as well as when and how to file it.

The board must also understand that fines often go unpaid, and fines do not guarantee a change in behavior. In many locations, late fees and interest may only be charged on the common assessment(s), so fines will just accumulate. Ultimately, those fines must be paid to clear the account before any sale of a home can be finalized, but that may be many, many years from the time of the infraction(s). Even suspension of certain privileges may not result in payment if the homeowner is not affected by the loss.

One thing the board must *absolutely never do* is to withdraw services that are mandated in the homeowner's agreement. It is inevitable that a board member, frustrated by the failure of a resident to pay their fines or cease their bad behavior, suggests the association should no longer shovel snow from their walkway or not include their home in a site wide painting project. The first action puts the association at risk of a liability lawsuit were an injury to result; the second harms the values of all of the surrounding homeowners. Board members need to come to terms with the fact that there is not always a solution to the problem at hand.

There is a saying in police work that everybody breaks the law multiple times each day without even realizing it. Yet, the police do not issue tickets or arrest every offender; they would have no time to apprehend more serious violators. In many ways, the board is in the same position. The vast majority of the residents are good people and will obey the regulations almost all the time. A handful will flaunt them. Concentrate on the truly bad apples, and leave more time to address the many other responsibilities of the board.

Insurance

Protecting the Association

ONE OF THE PRIMARY RESPONSIBILITIES of the board is to prevent harm to the association. One way to do so is by the use of insurance. The bylaws of the association often have specific instructions on what types of insurance must be carried by the association as well as what types must be carried by the homeowners. It is essential for the board to comply with the former and good practice for it to demand that the homeowners comply with the latter.

Association Requirements

General Liability and Umbrella

It is imperative that the board maintains adequate insurance on the common property and review the various policies on an annual basis. Typically, an association will have a master policy similar to a homeowner's policy. This will cover the association against common contingencies, such as fire or theft. Often the management agent will be familiar or have a relationship with a number of boutique insurers who specialize in homeowner associations. Do not be so fast to jump at a policy based on this specialization alone. Often times a traditional, full service insurance carrier (such as Allstate, Farmers and State Farm, to name but a few) will also quote the association a price on an identical or very similar policy that is lower than the specialist. Savings can be significant – $5,000 a year would not be uncommon. Of course, the property manager should review all quotes to make sure the coverages are identical and if not, how they differ.

There are a few things to be on the look out for when reviewing these policies. Is the association insuring unnecessary items, such as "fine art" in the association's clubhouse? The board must also pay close attention to per event and total coverages, how many events are allowed, as well as the deductible(s). If an insurance claim for the association is rare and it has adequate reserves, the annual savings from a higher annual deductible may pay off very quickly.

Any association that has a pool, gym, tennis courts or clubhouse definitely should carry the significant additional liability coverage provided by an "umbrella" policy. Be aware that even *trespassers* have been known to sue when injured on a property; for instance a pool hopper who tries to climb over a security fence falls and is injured. If a homeowner is sued due to personal injury to another person (or damage to their property) as the result of homeowner (in)action, the association, as the "big fish," may be named as an additional defendant in the suit. The association is a target for those and other similar claims that an umbrella policy can protect against at a reasonable cost. A conversation with the insurance agents and the property manager should give the board a good idea of the customary amounts of coverage for the association's size and amenities.

D&O

The board *must* carry Directors and Officers (D&O) insurance. This liability insurance indemnifies the entire board against suits brought by homeowners or outsiders, but it will not protect a board member if they break the law. The primary purpose of

D&O insurance is to pay for legal costs when defending a board member(s) against charges related to actual or alleged acts, misstatements, misleading statements, errors and omissions, breach of duty, neglect or more generally, ineptitude. Secondly, the D&O policy is used to indemnify the board against damages. Like other insurance, D&O polices vary both in the specifics of what is covered and the dollar limits payable against any claim(s). Be aware that, depending on the specifics of the claim, a D&O policy may pay for the legal defense of board members but *not* the damages that may be awarded to the complainant. In some cases, a claim against the D&O policy will be rejected and instead a claim for bodily injury or property damages will be made against the association's general liability policy.

An important. often neglected, aspect of D&O insurance is the issue of allocation of damages between negligent conduct and intentional conduct. This allocation is done by a jury or judge, if asked, at the time damages are to be awarded. Problems can occur when the D&O policy allows the insured (the HOA in this case) to retain the duty or right to defend and they then fail to request an allocation be made. In this event, it is possible for the D&O provider to walk from the damage claim as courts have ruled that the burden to determine the allocation (and thus what are and are not covered damages) lies with the insured. For this reason, it is a very good idea to request that the D&O policy include specific language to compel the insurer to associate in the defense of any claim against the HOA. As state laws vary, the board should have their attorney review this language to ensure that the burden of association is with the insurer and not the association.

Claims against volunteer boards (not just HOAs) have exploded in recent years, and with this rise has come a more diverse and complex landscape of coverage available under D&O policies. The board, in conjunction with the association's attorney and property manager, should undertake a thorough review of the association's existing coverage to determine if the policy in place is sufficient. If not, add coverage and the necessary riders or seek a new policy. Be warned that the board can even be sued for not obtaining adequate D&O insurance! Board members who are wealthy, or who feel they may be more vulnerable to a legal action, should inquire about a "Difference in Conditions" rider that will provide not just excess dollar coverage over the standard D&O policy but also fill gaps in that coverage. Skimping on D&O coverage to save a few hundred dollars is ill advised, not just because it opens up each board member to personal liability but because the association will have a harder time finding new volunteers to fill vacancies on the board.

Fidelity, Disability and Workers Compensation

Fidelity insurance is inexpensive and provides the association with additional coverage beyond the base liability policy for monetary losses due to dishonesty by officers, accountants and management agencies or theft by burglary. The treasurer should provide the board with an estimate of the maximum cash balance the association expects to have in its operational and reserve bank accounts (brokerage also, if they exist) during the calendar year. The board should then direct the property manager to obtain sufficient additional fidelity insurance to cover the peak balance. Failure to obtain this coverage will open the board to claims of negligence were theft or fraud to occur.

Finally, there are several smaller polices that the board should maintain as the cost is usually minimal. Even if the association has no employees of record on the association's payroll (e.g., a full-time handyman, a lifeguard, a night watchman), the board should maintain both disability and workers compensation coverage. These policies will protect the association if an employee of a contractor were injured while working on the property at a time the contractor's own insurance had lapsed or been revoked. Although the property manager will request proof of insurance from the various contractors who service the property, it is impractical to ask and wait for documentation prior to each and every visit (e.g., by an electrician fixing a broken light). As such, it is impossible for the association to be 100% certain at any given time that all contractors have adequate and necessary coverage. This leaves open the possibility that one of their employees, if injured, could sue the association to recoup medical expenses and other damages.

Homeowner Requirements

Many bylaws will also place specific requirements on the homeowners as to what kind of insurance must be carried, the amount of coverage and any additional qualifications. If the bylaws do not require insurance to be carried by the homeowners or do not address in sufficient details the specific requirements, the board should immediately form a subcommittee to draft an insurance policy for the association. The board must consider the association at risk until the policy is passed and all homeowners have complied.

The principal reason why the board must monitor homeowner insurance is simple – if one of the homes burns down, who will be responsible for rebuilding it? If the homes are not freestanding but part of a row, a fire can take out many homes at once. Again, who will pay for rebuild and when?

There are additional reasons as well. A visitor to a home can slip on a welcome mat while leaving to go home, fracturing their hip. The homeowner they visited has no liability insurance. With whom will the injured party file a claim? Don't think for a moment that they or their attorney will neglect to come after the HOA. Clearly, many liability related scenarios exist that can drag the HOA into the picture, primarily because the homeowner has no insurance and direct restitution from them via lawsuit could take a very long time if their primary asset is their home.

The first time a board implements an insurance policy, the members may be shocked to find not just homeowners without insurance but also homeowners with the wrong kind of insurance. Though it may be unfathomable how it can happen, some of the homeowners are likely to have condominium insurance instead of homeowner insurance *even though their mortgage was approved by a lender.* Condominium insurance does **not** provide for the rebuild of any portion of the structure, will replace only the damaged contents within the home, and provides only a small ($100,000 to $300,000) amount of liability coverage.

The board should begin the process with an understanding of typical homeowner polices. Though these policies usually cover against a myriad of things that can go wrong, the two most important items are the amounts of liability and rebuild coverage. Just as the association's insurance contains a general liability provision, so does the homeowner policy. The common floor is $300,000 and that may be increased to between $500,000 and $1,000,000 by the homeowner. Homeowner policies rarely provide more than $1,000,000 in liability (some carriers have a maximum of $500,000) and additional coverage is provided by an umbrella policy that picks up where other policies leave off (home or auto). It is not unusual for homeowners of higher valued properties and more personal wealth to carry umbrella policies providing $5,000,000 to $10,000,000 in excess liability protection.

The downside is the more coverage taken, the higher the annual cost to the homeowner. The board needs to determine what they feel is a fair minimum amount of general liability coverage that each homeowner should carry. At one time, $500,000 would probably suffice to cover most claims. In the current environment of litigation at the drop of a hat and staggering damage awards from juries, $1,000,000 is a better figure.

The rebuild provision of the policy is the most critical to the homeowner association. Three options are common in the industry at this time: cash value, replacement cost and extended replacement cost. Cash value will only pay the homeowner the estimated cost to replace the home *less depreciation.* Replacement cost basis will pay out funds to rebuild the home up to a stated dollar amount and no more. Extended replacement cost provides for an overage of a specified percentage (20% is normal) above replacement cost, if necessary, to complete the rebuild. Absolutely no homeowner should be allowed to insure for only cash value as the association can have no expectation that the homeowner will have sufficient additional funds to complete the rebuild in a timely manner, if at all, since depreciation will take a large chunk out of any settlement provided by the insurance company.

Although extended replacement cost is the ideal coverage, simple replacement cost with a reasonable estimation of the cost to rebuild is acceptable. The key, of course, is what is a reasonable cost of rebuilding the homes in the association? A good place to research that would be the board member's own policies and through a consultation with their insurance agents. With that information in hand, the board can take a simple average of the figures provided or even play it safe and take the highest one. Allowances can be made if there are multiple styles and sizes of homes in the association and a fair rebuild cost established for each.

Another beneficial item to add to the policy statement is a requirement that the association be named as an "additional insured." In effect, this extends the homeowner's liability policy to also protect the association. As an example: a homeowner's child leaves a skateboard outside on their walkway; a delivery person does not see it, trips and breaks their ankle. In this type of situation, any claim by the injured party is likely to go against both the homeowner and the association. The result should be a primary claim against the homeowner and a secondary claim against the association, with the association drawing first protection from the homeowner's policy as an additional insured.

In addition, any parties listed as additional insured will usually receive notification from the insurance company when changes are made to the policy, including cancellation. Unfortunately, not all carriers will allow a homeowner to name an additional insured to their policy. When reviewing the new insurance policy, the property manager may request that the management agency also be named as an additional insured. Reject this request. The goal the board is trying to achieve is the reduction of risk to all members of the association, not the management agency. The only time the management agency should be named as an additional insured is on a contractor's policy prior to the start of any work on the property that is to be overseen by the management agency. The board must also require that copies of the homeowner's insurance certificates be provided at least annually or when the carrier is changed.

On last item to be aware of is that not all insurers will extend the coverage in the homeowners policy to renters. This can mean that were there to be a fire or other liability event, the standard homeowner policy that is in place will not cover the event. The board must be sure to include in the final policy that if their home is rented, the homeowner must provide proof that their insurance will cover damages and liability while occupied by a tenant.

With the above in hand, the board subcommittee should draft the insurance policy statement for board approval, followed by distribution to the entire association. The policy statement should include the rational for the policy, explain the legitimacy of the board's actions in approving the new policy, and the specific homeowner requirements. Stumbling blocks with liability coverage are easily overcome by requiring some *total* amount of coverage between the base home policy and an associated umbrella policy. If the policy requires the association be named as additional insured, be sure to provide for the case of a carrier refusing the request by asking the homeowner to provide a written copy of the rejection from their agent/carrier. The cover letter to the homeowners should introduce the new policy and provide clear implementation details for the homeowner to follow (i.e. where to send copies of certificates).

The new policy will be impossible to implement unless the property manager and the management agency are also prepared to keep the necessary records and answer questions from homeowners about the policy. Most agencies are fully aware of the necessity of keeping track of these insurance records and may now do so for some of their properties. However, many will not voluntarily suggest to the board such a policy be implemented and enforced as it means a fair amount of paper work and record keeping for them. Therefore, the board must be very firm with the management agency, demanding that they do what is necessary in a timely manner to ensure compliance.

The board can expect pushback from homeowners. Some are certain to complain that it is too much work for them and others that the board is costing them money by requiring more coverage than they current carry. Ideally, the property manager should provide the board with a report detailing compliance with the policy at each board meeting. At a minimum, a summary statement should note how many homes are fully compliant, how many partially so, and how many not at all. The total of partially compliant homeowners should be broken down, if necessary, to show what requirement(s) they have failed to meet. A full backup statement listing the details of their insurance, such as the type, amount of coverage and expiration date should be available on request and provided without question quarterly (monthly, until most homeowners are in compliance). This report should also contain the date proof of insurance was received by the property manager as well as the date(s) reminder notices were sent to the homeowner. The latter is important; it assures the board that the property manager is requesting new certificates as policies expire and also helps the homeowner's comply in a timely manner.

The property manager will likely request that the reminders

go out quarterly so that they can group a large number together for one mailing. This is the minimally acceptable approach. Consider: a homeowner with a policy expiring the first month of the quarter will not receive a reminder for two months and will then be given up to an additional month to comply. This means some homeowners may be out of compliance for a full quarter, ignoring the additional risk the policy may have lapsed months earlier with no notice given to the association or the property manager. Request the property manager send the necessary reminders each month, but be prepared to compromise.

The board should not get their hopes up that the initial collection of certificates will be over quickly. Quite the contrary, it will likely take six to nine months before a point is reached where the list is stable, and the number of noncompliant homeowners is small. Often, those who do not comply will already be known as problem homeowners – either from rules infractions or being in arrears. Fines are generally less than effective with these cases (why pay a fine if one is not paying the common charge?) but the board does have additional options.

First, the property manager should determine from available records if the home was purchased using a mortgage. If so, the homeowner should be lettered informing them of the association's intention to notify their lender that they have not provided proof of insurance and suggesting the bank may wish to take out a policy on the home for its own protection. If the homeowner still refuses to comply, a cheap title search should be preformed to establish the current owner of the mortgage note (loans are often resold many times). The association's attorney can then be directed to contact the lender to advise them that the association believes the home may not be insured, that it must be insured to comply with the associations bylaws and regulations (with a copy of the requirements) and that the association requests the bank provide proof of insurance. If there is one thing which will motivate a lender, it is the fear they have lent against uninsured collateral. As every mortgage also requires insurance be kept in place on the home, the lender will be quick to either take a policy out on behalf of the homeowner or verify that there is, in fact, existing coverage in place. Either way, the association will have accomplished its goal of ensuring that the home has adequate and current coverage.

Second, the board can and should suspend all privileges of the non-complying homeowners. Of course, this only has meaning if the association has facilities, such as a pool, tennis courts or clubhouse. Even so, if the homeowner does not use these, there will be no effect. Note that if the unit is rented, suspension of pool rights will often lead to an angry exchange between the renter and homeowner, with the result the board does get proof of insurance.

Third, the board can publish or post a list of all noncompliant homeowners. To avoid appearances of bias or ganging up, the notice should also include how many have complied and how long the listed homeowners have been out of compliance. Although this may make the property manager uneasy, no personal financial information is revealed, and the nature of the notice is such that the information provided is rightly of great concern to the many other members of the association. Prior to publishing the notice, also discuss the issue with association's attorney, and have them review the document.

Unfortunately, one option the board does not have available is to purchase insurance on the homes of the homeowners who do not comply with the policy. Insurance companies require that the purchaser have a direct financial interest in the property covered, and although the association would certainly *seem* to have a financial interest, it does not in the eyes of the insurance industry. Frustratingly, even the argument that the association has the authority to compel the homeowner to effect repairs to the property (or be billed by the association for its cost to perform the work) does not move the insurance companies to allow the association to purchase coverage in lieu of the homeowner.

Finally, the board needs to establish a time table for compliance and a fine structure for failing to comply. It is regrettable that the mention of fines must be put up front, but without this threat a fair portion of homeowners will simply ignore the policy completely, even though it is for their own financial protection. During the initial phase, when the property manager is collecting the information for the first time, some leeway should be given to the homeowners. There may be confusion as to what is required, in part because the homeowner is not really familiar with insurance. Some may mail a copy of their policy instead of the actual certification of coverage. Many will contact their agent and request the documentation be sent (and perhaps changes be made to the underlying policies), but the information will never make it to the property manager. Sometimes this can be because the agent forgot or sent to the wrong e-mail address. E-mail can also be marked as junk (spam) and never make it to the intended recipient. Sometimes the management agency will be at fault. Faxes and letters may be misplaced, lost or thrown out. E-mail may be accidentally deleted or lost due to incorrect sorting.

Homeowners will be frustrated when they are told they remain out of compliance. This can happen if proof of insurance was indeed sent but the terms are incorrect, thus a back and forth with the property manager ensues. For these reasons, the board and property manager should attempt to detail the requirements in as simple language as possible, give definitions of terms homeowners may not be familiar and even provide copies of polices and certificates as examples to follow. The easier it is for the homeowner to get things right on the first try, the more likely the majority will comply in a timely manner initially and in the future.

Arrears

Getting Paid

JUST AS A BUSINESS DEPENDS UPON PAYMENT from their customers, so to does an HOA depend upon payment of common charges and assessments by the members of the association. For an association that has limited reserves, the failure of only a few to pay can lead to dire circumstances. If the association is unable to pay all of its bills, the day-to-day operations of the property may be affected. For better funded associations, large arrearages can lead to delays and postponements of necessary capital projects.

> *Throughout this chapter, references are made to legal and other actions that the board may elect to take against delinquent homeowners. Nothing within should be construed by the reader as legal advice specific to their association or that the possible actions discussed are legal in the jurisdiction of their association's property. Prior to taking any actions related to arrearages the board **MUST** consult with their association's attorney(s).*

Basic Policy

Many associations do not have a formal arrears policy detailing the type and timing of actions the board will take to clear an arrearage. Instead, an ad-hoc policy is used that leaves everyone guessing at what will be done and when. This type of case by case treatment may lead to legal problems for the association if homeowners are treated in significantly different ways for similar arrearages and accusations of favoritism arise.

Codifying an arrears policy is not difficult and should be a high priority for the board. The primary considerations are when the following events should occur:

- reminder letter from property manager

- warning letter from attorney

- lien placed on the property

- second warning from attorney

- filing of foreclosure papers

Timing can be based upon a set number of months (or quarters) the homeowner is delinquent or the basis can be a dollar amount of arrears. Generally, it is best to combine both as this simplifies the handling of arrears with unpaid assessments, fines, legal charges, late fees and interest.

The setting of dollar amounts is dependent on the base common charge, what percentage ownership each unit has in the association, the cost to file a lien and last, the cost to file a foreclosure and see the entire process through the court system.

If the base common charge is low, the time period before each action will be somewhat longer than at a higher fee association. This is to take into account the relative cost of time spent writing letters, consulting with attorneys and filing legal documents compared to the dollar amount of the outstanding arrearage.

On the other hand, in a small association, say 25 units, the loss of 4% of common charge income is potentially significant as the board cannot assume only one member will be in arrears at any given time. In this situation, though the process may not be accelerated, it is quite likely the board will want hard and fast dates to apply, regardless of the actual dollar amount of the arrearage.

In most cases, the property manager will contact the delinquent homeowner with a reminder after two consecutive nonpayments. After three or four months, the association's attorney will send a letter to the homeowner informing them a lien will be placed on their property in 30 days if they do not pay or make some other arrangement with the board. The property manager will follow-up with the attorney 30 days later to advise them that there has been no change; the attorney will then file a lien after the appropriate officer(s) of the board sign-off on the documents. The lawyer will again letter the homeowner with notice of the intention of the association to begin foreclosure proceedings using the previously granted lien. Typically, this will happen two or three months after the date the lien proceedings began. This allows the courts time to process that paper work and also provides additional time for the homeowner to clear the arrearage. As foreclosures are not cheap, the association should also be sure the monies involved are sufficient to justify the filing. An example of an arrears policy is shown in *Appendix A*.

It will be necessary for the board to debate the above issues and reach a consensus with the help of the property manager. Note that even though the example policy does set out a detailed process for handling arrears, it also allows the board to take other actions it deems appropriate. For instance, the board can be approached by a homeowner with a request to establish a payment plan that may temporarily reduce their common charge. A homeowner who has just lost their job may only be able to pay 50% of the common charge each month. It is better for the board to accept that, reach an accommodation on the duration of the reduction and set a term for the repayment of the arrearage, than to continue to demand 100%. The board may elect to wave or adjust late fees or the interest rate on the outstanding balance. The board must, however, be careful when working with homeowners on payment plans that the terms offered are comparable for similar financial situations. Terms should be formally recorded by the property manager, recorded in the executive session minutes and referenced as new cases develop.

The proposed policy should be thoroughly reviewed by the association's attorney to be sure no federal or state statutes are violated, such as by charging too high a rate of interest or late fee. The late fee must not be so large as to be considered punitive by the courts, but it can still be large enough to get the point across, say $35-$50 a month. The interest rate should be set at the highest rate allowed by law, but rates vary *dramatically* from state to state and in some cases are not capped. In the absence of a maxium rate, the board should consider using the typical credit card cash advance rate.

Once the board has the policy approved, it should be distributed to all of the homeowners, the management agency and the association's attorney. The cover letter should explain the need for the policy and urge any homeowners experiencing financial difficulties to contact the board.

Enforcement

Unfortunately, the arrears policy is great in principle but often fails to deliver in the most difficult circumstances. The conclusion is that our legal system makes it exceedingly difficult and expensive to collect from delinquent homeowners.

Along with the other financial reports sent to board members each month, there is an arrears report showing all members of the association with past due balances. This report is only an indicator of the true situation as it suffers from many payment timing issues. The property manager should be required to bring an updated copy the night of the regular board meeting, ideally after the 15th of the month or whatever day is used as a cut-off to determine when an account is late. That report will reflect only the true past due balances.

Without doubt, there are homeowners who are late simply because they forgot to mail the check in time or have some other short term issue. There are also homeowners who are regularly in arrears but almost always clear them before any action is taken to place a lien on their property. As long as they continue to pay off the balance, these delinquents are in fact the association's best customers as they pay interest and late fees almost every month.

The difficult decisions for the board come when the time to file a foreclosure nears. Prior to this point, the association's attorney should have researched the property. Is there a mortgage note? Are there any tax or other liens on the property besides the association's? What is the estimated market value of the home and approximately what principal balance remains on any mortgage note? Has the board had any contact at all with the homeowner?

Depending on the answers to those questions, the board may be entering a foreclosure with a realistic hope of recovering what the association is owed (plus legal and other expenses) or one simply to expedite the day a new, paying homeowner takes over the property, conceding the hope of any recovery. Some board members may bristle at the latter course of action, but the sooner the arrearage is identified as a sunk cost, ultimately the better off the association will be financially.

The association's attorney should explain in detail the local regulations governing foreclosures. The municipality and other government agencies are always paid first. Next, the mortgage holder, then the association. In most cases, if any of those superior parties files their own foreclosure after, but prior to the resolution of the association's filing, they will move ahead of the association and the foreclosure clock is, in effect, reset.

If there is no mortgage, the board is in some luck. It should explore the purchase of any outstanding tax liens on the property from the local municipality. Tax liens, which can also be used to foreclose on a property, are generally considered an investment; some bylaws may restrict such purchases. Regardless, it is possible that the association may be able to foreclose prior to the local government filing their claim as some municipalities wait up to 36 months before filing a foreclosure against the homeowner.

If there is a mortgage and there appears to be positive equity in the property, the association may be able to recover the complete arrears owed. If the property is underwater, the sooner the association files the foreclosure the better. If there are other liens on the property, it is unlikely the homeowner intends to pay the association or anyone else. As a foreclosure can take over two years to complete, every month wasted in debate is another month's common charge the association may never see.

If another party files the foreclosure, the board must make sure its attorney files the necessary paperwork with the courts as an interested party. This will ensure that the association is notified of any and all important changes or milestones in the case as they occur.

The association's attorney may recommend getting a financial judgment prior to going to foreclosure. A judgment can be used to seize and sell assets or garner wages. The thought here is that the association is able to use the judgment regardless of the current ownership of the property. This presumes that there are other assets, such as cars, that do not already have liens which the association may seize and sell. Likewise, if the owner is not working or the association is unable to determine where they do work, garnishing wages can be difficult. In addition, garnishing is subject to limitations as well as precedence, such as child support. Another headache occurs when the homeowner works in a neighboring state which then necessitates further legal work to enforce the judgment. Bank accounts can be seized, but they may be difficult to find, and the homeowner is unlikely to leave any substantial balance in the accounts. They realize that not only the association, but the IRS, governmental agencies and other creditors are probably looking to take this money as well.

Cars, which are not leased and are paid off, may be seized if titled to the homeowner. If the association is lucky, the auction value of the car may bring in a few thousand dollars. Unfortunately, in these types of situations the car will often be older, and the auction value may not exceed the cost to have the sheriff seize it. Even so, claiming the car at a small loss may still have value to the board as a symbolic deterrent to other homeowners with more attractive assets.

In theory, a judgment can be sold or given to a third party for collection, though in both cases the association gives up a substantial portion of any award recovery, with no assurance anything will be collected at all.

For all of those reasons, avoid the time and effort to seek a court ordered judgment unless the association's attorney and property manager are quite certain they will be able to easily collect a substantial portion of the award.

One unique situation occurs when the homeowner who is in arrears leases their property to a tenant. Though rules vary from state to state, the association may be able to *legally* direct the tenant to pay any rent monies due to the homeowner directly to the association until such a time as the arrearage is cleared. In some cases, the tenant may be very upset to be contacted by the association's attorney. Their complaints alone can result in the homeowner paying off the arrearage promptly, rather than risk the tenant breaking their lease and the resulting loss of income that would entail.

The board must be careful in the actions they take as well as the statements they make in regards any arrears problem to avoid conflicts with regulations, such as the "Fair Debt Collection Practices Act." Other than the possible suspension of privileges to use common area facilities, the homeowner should be treated no differently than any other member of the association. The last thing the board needs is to give the offending homeowner an easy lawsuit victory that costs the association even more money. One recourse the board has, however, is to publish notice of liens and foreclosures in the association's regular newsletter after they have been formally filed with the local court system. All the information contained in those documents are part of the public record.

> *Throughout this chapter references are made to legal and other actions which the board may elect to take against delinquent homeowners. Nothing within should be construed by the reader as legal advice specific to their association or that the possible actions discussed are legal in the jurisdiction of their association's property. Prior to taking any actions related to arrearages the board **MUST** consult with their association's attorney(s).*

The Property

THE PROPERTY OF THE ASSOCIATION can be broadly divided into three groups: facilities, structures and grounds. Every association will have structures and grounds but may not have facilities. We define facilities to include pools, tennis courts, clubhouses, fitness or workout rooms, and similar which are commonly owned and managed by the board on behalf of the entire association. Structures are defined broadly as buildings which may be common or homeowner property. The grounds include both properties deemed common and those deeded directly to the homeowner.

Unlike traditional homes located on deeded property, units within the association, though also deeded, may carry certain restrictions as defined in the homeowners' agreement. As a result, the board will have instances when they must make decisions that will have an impact on homeowner property and not just on the common areas. The homeowners' agreement may specify certain areas in which the unit owner may landscape his or her property and others where the association is responsible. The association may also be responsible for maintenance and repair of certain portions of the physical structure of the homes, often the roof, and the board is permitted to make rules which limit the rights of the homeowners to change or modify their homes.

The Facilities

Facilities are a mixed blessing for an association. If well maintained, they can increase the value of the members' homes but if allowed to run down, they will not only become an eyesore but will turn off prospective buyers. Facilities can also cause friction within the community. Pools, courts and gyms are not cheap to maintain and staff, and this expense will be shared by all owners even though only a small fraction of the membership will use them. The board will likely find that only a quarter to a half of homeowners will make any regular use of a pool, the one facility most likely to have good attendance. Tennis and other courts get far less attention and may only be used by a small clique of homeowners. Workout facilities will see use dependent upon both the demographics of the association and the extent they are viewed as an adequate replacement for a dedicated gym membership.

The Pool

From a board perspective, the pool is likely to be the facility that causes the most aggravation. There will always be some issue or problem with the pool. Some will say that it would be better filled with sand than water!

In most climates the pool will open around Memorial Day weekend but in the Deep South or Southwest the pool may be a year-round endeavor. The property manager should be familiar with local, county and state regulations pertaining to the operation of the pool and should be able to handle or arrange much of the work which goes into its operation. The board should be familiar with the entire process; at the least to stay on top of the management agency and at the worst to be able to handle the job when necessary. One board member should always be designated to oversee the pool operations and act as the property manager's primary liaison.

The annual pool process begins with the required permitting of the facility, essentially a paperwork exercise with a government agency, such as the board of health. A permit should be requested at the earliest date possible to leave time to correct errors or omissions and still receive approval prior to the planned opening date. No board wants is residents with pitchforks at the next meeting because the pool is not opened by the expected or traditional date.

After the permit come decisions on the day-to-day upkeep and operation of the pool. There are two major decisions to be made by the board: Will the pool be "swim at your own risk" or guarded? If guarded, will the board hire a single lifeguard or contract with a pool management company for guard services? Before making a decision to go with an at your own risk pool, the board needs to consult with its property manager, attorney and insurance company.

First, the property manager should speak with the local regulatory body to determine if the pool can even be granted at your own risk status. In some localities, an on duty lifeguard is mandatory for certain pool depths, dimensions and bather capacity. The association's attorney will be able to offer guidance on legal case history in the state with respect to accidents and other issues at an unguarded pool. They should also be able to advise the board and its property manager what notifications must be made to absolve the association of as much liability for incidents at the pool as possible. Finally, the association will, of course, have an insurance policy (covered more in the *Insurance* chapter), and the board should ask the carrier for rates on all three options as money may be a factor in the ultimate decision.

If the board decides to go without a guard, it should be sure to have the appropriate signage in place prior to opening the pool and a person responsible for verifying that the signs are not removed or otherwise damaged during the season. If this will be a change from a pool with a lifeguard, residents must be notified of the change and the reasons why the board made this decision. Expect to be asked about liability risks and hear homeowner concerns over lawsuits. The unguarded pool, when allowed by local regulations, is probably a cost-effective solution for a small association, especially in a resort area where owners come and go and are not full-time residents. It is probably not appropriate, even if allowed, for a large association that sees heavy and regular use of the pool by full-time residents.

Once a decision is made to have a guard at the pool, the board will need to hire one. Even though guards may be hired individually, a pool management company is the better choice. Most lifeguards are college or high school students and cannot be expected to be 100% reliable. Excuses will vary, but even the best guards will be late or absent at least a few days during the summer. Unless the association has a backup they can call on short notice, the pool will need to remain closed on those days. This might not be a major issue on a Monday or Tuesday, but is certain to cause considerable grumbling by the residents if a beautiful Saturday is missed.

On the other hand, a pool management company is in the business of running pools and thus will have a large staff of lifeguards. Procedures vary, but a good company will have the assigned guard call into their office from a phone at the association's pool. The company will have this phone number on record so as to be able to verify the guard really is where they claim to be. If a guard does not show up for any reason, another can be dispatched, or as a last resort, one of the managers can fill in. The pool management company will also train the guards in basic pool maintenance and inform them of any "house rules" which should be followed at the pool. If the board has issues with a guard, it is easy to call a manager to have the problem corrected or a new guard assigned to the property.

Another benefit of using a pool management company is that they will also arrange for chemical deliveries, check equipment, make minor repairs and handle any issues which may come up during a state or local pool inspection. The alternative is for the board to hire individual guards and arrange for chemical deliveries and maintenance by a pool service company. The latter option will require far more board oversight and involvement in the day-to-day operation of the pool, and the cost savings, if any, may not be material. However, if the pool and association are small, this may be the more practical alternative.

The board should get bids from two or three pool management companies, estimates of the cost and availability of local guards, and the cost of a pool service only contract. Due diligence is extremely important – saving a few thousand dollars but ending up with unprofessional guards is not a road any board should travel. Ask for references from the management companies as well as individual guards, if that option is under consideration. The board should also inquire how staffing is handled late in the season (early September) or during the school year if the pool is open most of the year.

Most pool rules are standardized, and widely available signage should be posted as necessary to meet state and local regulations, as well as to protect the association from liability risk. The local regulatory body or the pool management company will be able to assist the board and management agent to ensure no points have been missed. The board should also give strong consideration to creating pool rules and regulations to supplement those that are mandated by law. Rules must be distributed to the residents of the association prior to the opening of the pool and it is advisable to keep a copy on hand with the on-duty guard in case of questions or problems with a resident or guest.

Some of the most contentious issues which must be addressed in the pool rules is: who can use the pool, under what circumstances and when? Is the pool to be owner and residents only? If guests are to be allowed, how many at any one time? How many during a given day or week? Can the guest(s) be left alone at the pool? Will there be a charge for guests? Is there an age restriction on use of the pool? Must parents or caregivers be present when children use the pool and if so, through what age? If young children are allowed, must they wear certain protective clothing? What are the regular operating hours/days of the pool? Is swim at your own risk ever permitted and under what conditions? Will there be an adult swim period? Each of those is a potential minefield for the board to navigate, in particular if coming from a situation where a pool has been run chaotically or with lax enforcement of rules. Whatever choices are made, there will be pushback; the board should be prepared to stand firm by their decisions. Modifications to the rules should not be considered until the next season.

The guest rules in particular cause great distress because they are the most abused (or ignored). Few people will be happy to arrive at their pool to find most of the space occupied on a regular basis by one resident's guests or extended family. Though first come, first served, the pool is a limited, shared resource and some effort must be made to put residents first and guests second. Placing a reasonable limitation on the number of guests one resident may bring to the pool at any given time or cumulatively over some period, provides a good check on this kind of abuse. A small fee can also be charged for guests beyond a certain number and the money used to purchase pool supplies or accessories.

Another sore point is owners and residents with parents or adult children they wish to allow the use of the pool. This type of behavior should not be permitted. The association is not running a pool club for non-residents. As an example, a grown son or daughter of an owner should not be allowed to use the pool on the way home from work as a guest while the owner is still at work or elsewhere. This will naturally lead into a discussion of "Must the owners or residents be present at the pool while their guest is using the facility?" The answer should be yes. Beyond assuring the guest privilege is not abused, there are practical reasons for this rule. Who is responsible for the behavior of the guest? What if a guest is injured and has no identification but a guest pass?

Identification passes and a sign-in book should be used at all pools. Passes allow the guard to establish that the person coming to the pool actually is a resident or guest of the association. Unless the property is a secure, gated compound, do not for a moment discount the possibility of outsiders trying to use the association's facility. Some may even have been encouraged to do so by association residents! The board should periodically check that the lifeguards are enforcing the sign-in and guest rules and make sure that pen, not pencil, is used. It may be shockingly petty, but at least some of the residents will try to modify the number of guests in their party to skirt the rules or avoid fees. The sign-in book is a valuable resource in its own right. The board can use it to evaluate pool usage patterns and align the hours of the pool to achieve a good balance of availability versus operational costs. Savings can be banked or even applied against the cost of adding extra days to either end of the pool season.

At least one resident is certain to ask the board to open the pool early in the morning, perhaps before work. Unless the pool can be operated on an at your own risk basis in whole or in part, the board will not be able to accommodate this request as it is cost prohibitive. Far more likely to be acceptable are requests to extend the pool hours to better accommodate commuting residents, even if for only one night a week.

Other rules to consider relate to personal conduct. Are pool games allowed and, if so, when and what kind? What kinds of beverages are allowed at the pool and in what type of containers? (Glass containers are almost universally prohibited due to the risk of broken pieces going into the pool water.) Is food allowed? If there is an attached clubhouse, are wet bathing suits permitted inside the clubhouse? Where? Is smoking or cell phone use permitted? What is the penalty for failing to follow the pool rules? Failure to follow the lifeguard's instructions?

Finally, the security of the pool is very important. The board must understand that the pool represents a serious liability risk and appropriate measures must be in place to constrain access to the pool to only those who are approved by the board to use it and only during the posted hours of operation. All pools should be fenced in at the maximum height allowed by local ordinances to prevent neighboring children or other "pool hoppers" from attempting to swim during off hours. From a liability standpoint, a locked pool is the best pool, and all access points should be locked or chained when the pool is closed. If the pool is not staffed by a lifeguard, it will be impractical to lock overnight. However, the handles on entrance gates can be positioned high enough so as to discourage or prevent access by small children. The board should ask the property manager or pool company to check the perimeter on a regular basis and remove or adjust items which can be used to assist in climbing over the security fence as well as verify that all gates and locks are functional.

If the pool fencing is old, too low or just unsightly, consideration should be given to replacement. There are a number of styles available in aluminum fencing which are more difficult to climb than chain link, and provide a visual upgrade that can translate into higher home resale values. The cost of materials and installation will run from $10,000 to $20,000 for the average pool and deck area.

Any discussion of a pool would be remiss to not briefly touch on pool furniture. There will be some board members who only consider the look of tables and chairs and ignore or discount other practical considerations. One that should not be brushed off is the choice of glass tops for the tables. Though it is pleasing to the eye, glass should be avoided. Even assuming a pool is secure from vandalism, there is little the board can do to prevent storm or accidental damage to the tables. If any glass gets into the pool, it may need to be drained and cleaned at not insignificant expense – water in the amounts required to fill an in-ground pool can cost several thousand dollars. Though other tabletop material choices are preferable, if glass is chosen, keep the tables a safe distance from the edge of the pool and be sure to move them well away if a severe storm is expected. (Don't forget to store the umbrellas too!)

At the end of the season, the pool service or management company will do routine work on the pool and place a cover on top. Water is normally left in the pool, even in cold climates, but the board may need to have a plumber come in to properly drain various pipes before winter begins. The pool company should also arrange for the stacking and storage of tables, chairs and umbrellas. If possible, umbrellas should be kept indoors along with any seat cushions to prolong their useful life. Tarps used to cover the furniture should be securely tied down or weighted. The property manager should verify that the work has been completed satisfactorily and then periodically check to make sure the tarps and pool cover are still restrained during the winter months and after severe storms.

Courts

The association may also have tennis courts, most likely of the outdoor variety. Depending on demographics and weather, the courts may see a lot of use or next to nothing. Because tennis must be played in pairs or doubles, the primary users of the facility are likely to be a clique. The board should try to gauge the usage of the courts for maintenance and repair purposes and to establish a scheduling mechanism.

If the courts are heavily used, the board may adopt a more formal mechanism for residents to schedule time to play than a simple first come, first served process. A public sign-up sheet with a week or two of time slots should be kept in an accessible location, in ink and out of the elements. This should satisfy all but the busiest facility if properly honored by residents.

If the courts are not open year-round, the board will need to establish the tennis court season. Many associations will tie the pool and tennis court dates together, but as tennis can be played in cooler weather, the board can certainly allow the courts to remain open into late fall. Winter maintenance is usually just the removal and storage of the nets and any privacy screening on perimeter fencing with the reverse in the spring. Also in the spring, the court surfaces will be reconditioned as necessary. If the courts are very heavily used, it may be necessary to have more frequent care of the surface.

A perennial question with regards to tennis courts is whether they should be locked when not in use. There are a few reasons to lock the courts: use past recommended hours disturbs nearby residents; vandalism; use for non-tennis activities after hours, frequently by teenagers. If the association does not have these concerns, by all means, leave the courts unlocked as it is far easier on everyone.

If locking is necessary, the board will then need to determine who will handle the daily opening and closing of the courts. It should not be board members or other residents because their reliability cannot be ensured. The management agency will not wish to make a special trip twice a day to do this chore either. Thus, the most likely candidate to handle this task will be one of the lifeguards at the pool (assuming there are both types of facilities). This will constrain the tennis court hours to be approximately the same as the pool and will undoubtedly cause friction with at least some residents who wish to use the courts at another time. But until the board has a resolution of the issues that led to the lockdown, the reduced hours must stand. If the courts are not open year-round, once the season has ended they should be locked to prevent unauthorized use and possible damage during the off-season.

Just as a pool has rules, so too should the tennis courts, and they should be posted courtside as well as distributed each year to the residents. Items to consider are acceptable match length, attire and footwear, and how many courts may be in use at one time by the same resident and guests, to name but a few. A fine system should be known and in place to address unauthorized use of the courts, such as playing with pets, baseball practice and other non-tennis related activity. Do not underestimate the ability of the residents to find new uses for the tennis courts, including as a dog run!

Gym

Gyms or workout rooms are usually only found in large associations or those in a resort area. Most will have an assortment of aerobic equipment (bikes, stairs, ellipticals, treadmills) and possibly some weight lifting equipment. The latter is almost always limited to "universal" style equipment so as to avoid the need for a spotter and minimize the risks of lifting weights without one present. Many will also have a selection of dumbbells which can be used for weight training or to accentuate an aerobic workout.

When deciding on how to spend funds on such a facility, the board should have a good idea of how much use it gets, which machines are used and which are not (assuming all are in proper working order) and any reasonable requests from the residents for additional equipment. A sign-in sheet or other mechanism to record visits to the gym is a good way to see how much use the gym gets, when, and by whom. If the facility does not get much use, or only by a handful of residents, it will be difficult to justify significant expenditures, either in absolute terms or relative to other facilities, such as pool and tennis courts. It may even be more practical to convert the space into some other use that more residents would value.

When looking at usage statistics, be careful to consider the full year period as activity can be seasonal in some climates. Access to the facility can also be a significant determinant of how often it is used. If most of the homeowners and residents work weekdays and the gym is only open 9–5, it will never see much use. The good thing about a gym is that a card key lock can be installed allowing 24/7 access to the residents, provided an outside or secure indoor entrance is available. If the gym is part of a larger clubhouse, the board will need to consider if unfettered access is desirable or if another entrance with more limited access can be made available to reach the gym If the facility is to be a new addition, access considerations must be part of the planning to maximize the association's investment. And like a pool or tennis court, a guest policy is also necessary.

There will always be some request for equipment which is just outside of the association's budget or is in excess of what is appropriate to spend based on usage. In these cases, the board can either deny the request outright or offer to contribute some fraction of the cost as a middle ground. The shortfall can be made up by contributions from those who would use the equipment most. Also likely are requests for TVs with cable/satellite. At one time the cost of a TV set would place it in the luxury category, but today LCD flat-screen sets of 32" can be purchased for about $350. The more difficult cost to absorb is the monthly cable or satellite subscription, which can easily run $600 to $1,200 per year. Even though a DVD or BluRay® player may be a cheaper option, care must be taken to ensure that the content played is appropriate for all audiences.

Clubhouse

Most mid- and larger-sized associations will have a clubhouse or other building for the use of all residents. Some are pretty spartan affairs; others may be more generously equipped to handle anything from club meetings to game rooms. If available and large enough, the board will use one of the rooms for its regular meetings and for the annual meeting of homeowners too. As the clubhouse is common property, the board must take care of the upkeep and maintenance of the building as well as setting rules for its use.

The property manager should arrange for a cleaning service on a regular basis that is conditioned on the use of the building. For example, seasonal clubhouses may need weekly cleanings in the summer and little or no attention in winter months. The property manager should also ensure the cleaning service is paying close attention to the restrooms as residents will complain loudly and often to the board if these are not kept clean.

The clubhouse could also be suitable for parties and other group entertainment. Procedures should be in place for the rental of the entire clubhouse or certain rooms by homeowners or residents. These should include a signed rental agreement making them financially responsible for the prompt cleaning, removal of refuse and any damages to the area used. A refundable deposit should be held in escrow, and the renters should be required to obtain what is commonly called "event" insurance, which costs $50 to $100 per one million dollars of liability coverage. This insurance is to protect the association should there be an incident which results in a lawsuit, such as a fall or a drinking while driving accident after the event.

If clubs will be regular users of the clubhouse, the board should ask the property manager in conjunction with the association's attorney to create a term contract, to be signed by all club members, that is not onerous to them yet protects the association. Unfortunately, we live in a very litigious society, and the last thing the board and association members want to hear is "We didn't think that would be necessary."

If the clubhouse is connected to a pool facility, the rental contract should specify that the pool may only be used under a separate signed agreement stipulating the rental group must arrange with the property manager to have lifeguard service during the event and at their own expense. Pool rules and regulations should also be provided with the understanding that the lifeguard has final say in all matters and may terminate use of the pool when necessary to avoid undue risk. The lifeguard should also be authorized to contact the local police, if necessary, as well as one of the officers of the board and the property manager.

The board may be asked to authorize the use of the clubhouse by a homeowner or group to sell items or services. Here the decision-making becomes a bit tricky. First, ignoring all other considerations, is the board comfortable at all with the notion of commercial use of the facility? Are inside groups acceptable, but not outsiders? This is a decision for which the board should be unanimous, or nearly so, as it is a move beyond what most would consider the traditional use of a clubhouse for the recreation and enjoyment of the homeowners.

A good idea is to amend the usage policy to specify that any commercial use will be at the sole discretion of the board. This allows an out should there be an event proposed that may prove offensive to some residents or is, for some other reason, less than desirable. The board should also consult with their insurance carrier to verify that such use of the facility will not in any way reduce or invalidate the association's current coverages (that are in addition to any which the renter is required to purchase). A consultation with the association's attorney is also advisable.

Some additional points to consider include: Will the event result in significant traffic through the property? Is there adequate space? Will turnout be so large that there is an outsized risk of damages to the building or surrounding grounds? Will the event cause undue aggravation to owners living nearby? As the event is commercial, will the board charge a per event or hourly rate?

Structures

THOUGH THE ASSOCIATION IS CLEARLY RESPONSIBLE for common buildings, such as a clubhouse, guardhouse or storage and utility shacks, the homeowners' agreement will explain what responsibilities the association may have for the repair and maintenance of homeowner structures. Rarely, however, does the agreement include all items which by common sense it should, and the board may find that it needs to formally take charge of certain responsibilities in the best interests of all the homeowners.

For the purpose of this discussion, items that are routinely handled by the board will be covered, and no assumptions are made regarding any particular association's responsibilities. Please remember that even in cases where the association has no *financial* responsibility, the board will almost certainly have to develop guidelines and procedures for homeowner sponsored repairs and maintenance and under what circumstances such work is required. Often, a large factor in determining what the board is and is not on the hook for is whether the association is made of individual free standing homes or is comprised of a series of attached ("row") homes.

Roof

Starting at the top, the association may be responsible for the maintenance, repair and replacement of shingles on the roof of the homes. The typical life of a shingled roof is 20 to 30 years but can vary with the quality of the materials used and installation methods. Homeowners will frequently complain of leaks and attempt to have the association pay for repairs to the roof and any inside damages. However, many roof issues can be traced back to problems with flashing rather than the shingles. Over time, though, shingles may come loose or detach during storms exposing the tar paper and decking beneath to the elements.

Shingle damage, once known, should be fixed as soon as possible to prevent any significant water damage either to the decking or the interior of the homes. If the problem is traced to flashing and this is not one of the association's responsibilities, the board must compel the homeowner to perform the necessary repairs so as to prevent damage to shingles or other elements which *are* association responsibility.

The property manager should inspect the roof from ground level at least annually and a roofer should be called in as necessary to fix any problems seen. Do not rely upon recovering costs based upon a warranty which came with the roof. Most will prorate over the life of the roof and will cover materials only. For this reason, any capital project to replace roofing should place heavy weight on the reputation of the material manufacturers and the contractor doing the installation. In addition to being a significant capital cost, any shortcuts taken to save money or time may haunt the association for decades to come. As noted earlier, flashing may or may not be an association responsibility when it comes to repairs but will be included as part of a roof replacement.

When doing capital budgeting, it is important to have already determined if the building structures are capable of taking the load of a second roof. The board should not rely upon their property manager to make this determination. An error can result in the association finding they have under or over reserved by many hundreds of thousand dollars. Instead, the board should seek an outside opinion by a certified architect or engineer who is familiar with the details of the local building codes. The management agency should also stay abreast of building code changes and report to the board on any that can have a material effect on the association's reserves.

Fireplaces

If the homes have fireplaces, homeowners will at some point ask when the association is going to clean or recap them. The answer is almost certain to be never. Though a condominium association is likely required to take care of this on their own initiative, it is rarely a mandated HOA responsibility. The board should, however, instruct the property manager to send out a periodic reminder to the homeowners noting that the responsibility for upkeep is theirs as well as the responsibility for any damages caused by neglect. The same reminder should also recommend the cleaning of dryer vent lines which accumulate lint over time and are quite quick to catch fire given a chance. In older developments, the board may also wish to remind residents that flexible plastic or foil vent lines are now considered to be risky, and replacement with rigid or flexible aluminum metal is recommended.

Skylights

Some homes have skylights, which are usually a homeowner responsibility. During a roof replacement, the board may determine that these skylights should be replaced simultaneously either for aesthetic or practical reasons (age may prevent a secure re-installation). If all homes have a similar number, the cost of replacement can be included in the total project cost and be taken out of common funds.

More difficult will be the case when only some homes have the skylights. In that case the board will not be able to split the cost equally and instead will need to charge back to the individual homeowner for the cost directly tied to their home.

> Any time there are charge backs for work done by the association, the board must expect questions about the necessity of repairs or replacements. It should be prepared for potential legal action by homeowner(s) who do not wish to be forced to make the repairs or assume the associated cost. There must be a compelling reason to force repairs or replacements on unwilling homeowners.

The board can also explore the the practicality of closing the opening from the existing skylight, and offer this as an alternative option to the homeowner. Of course, this may not be well-received either.

Miscellaneous Roof/Attic Issues

What about homeowner modifications to the roof? There are two common cases: addition of a satellite dish and installation of an attic vent fan. At one time, homeowner and condominium associations had absolute control over antenna and dishes for radio and TV reception. But with the growth in small dish satellite systems like DIRECTV®, the Federal Communications Commission passed regulations that prevent these associations from placing outright bans on such reception equipment. Instead, the regulations mandate the board to develop reasonable rules and restrictions on the use and placement of antennae.

The board should formulate specific guidelines on the placement and size of antennas and incorporate them with the complete rules and regulations of the association. Satellite dishes should not be installed on the roof. Poor installation may compromise the water barrier, and the board has no way to verify the ability and quality of individual installers. Instead, install the dish on the side of a chimney structure (if one exists) or on the side of the building. If homes have a utility shed, it too can be used if it points in the correct direction for reception. The board should also discourage the placement of a dish over the front facing door (or windows) of a home for aesthetic reasons.

Homeowners may also have interest in installing an attic vent fan to assist in cooling their homes during the summer months. This will require the cutting of the roof to install the fan and possibly the siding for another vent below the eaves to provide additional airflow. The board does not have to allow these requests but if they do, specifications should be given to all homeowners regarding the size, color and shape of the fan. Also stipulate that the homeowners will be responsible for any

damages to the roof in the vicinity of the fan and also any resulting water or insect damage inside the home. If the association
has homeowner committees, the architecture committee can
help establish some of the required specifications.

Gutters and Leaders

Gutters and leaders may be overlooked in the homeowners'
agreement. If so, and the association is comprised of attached
homes, the board should undertake the cleaning, repair and, if
necessary, replacement of these items. If the homes are freestanding individual units, unless otherwise specified, the board
need not assume this maintenance role but it will be practical
to do so. Freestanding or not, if and when the time comes to
replace the gutters and leaders, the board should assume full
control for purposes of maintaining uniformity among all the
homes.

   Though seemingly a simple thing to maintain, failure to
do so properly can lead to a host of water related problems –
peeling or moldy paint, rotted siding, flooding in and around
the homes are but a few. Depending on the type, number and
proximity of trees, as well as the climate, cleanings may be
required multiple times a year. In colder climates two cleanings
are usually done, the first after flowers and other spring season
detritus have fallen and the second a few weeks after most leaves
have dropped from the trees, usually some time in November.
The property manager can make arrangements with a company
which specializes in gutter cleaning and repair but a competent
handy man may be used in small and midsized developments.

   Although all boards are concerned with costs, consideration
should also be given to the thoroughness and cleanliness of the
contractor. It does no good to save a few hundred dollars if
someone else must be hired to clean up patios, decks and the
grounds around the homes from debris tossed out of the gutters.
Mud can be flung onto the sides of the home and if not washed

off promptly, can stick when dry requiring much more effort to clean off. Along with the gutters, the downspouts into the leaders must be checked for debris and clogging. Failure to do this may negate the benefit of cleaning out the gutters entirely. Likewise, the pitch of the gutters should be checked from time to time to ensure proper water flow.

> Whenever work crews will be on the roof or working on ladders around the upper windows of the homes, the board should make sure the management agency posts or sends a notice to the homeowners with the approximate date and time the work will be done. This will hopefully prevent any unfortunate incidents between homeowners in their bedrooms and workers near those windows!

Siding, Trim and Paint

Next comes the main part of each building – the siding, trim and paint. The approach here is to describe the elements of a typical painting project which can be adapted if other materials are used. Painting projects are one of the top three regular capital expenditures many associations will incur and when viewed cumulatively, are probably the single biggest outlay. The board should extend all possible efforts in conjunction with the property manager to do the work properly. Failure to do so can result in reduced home values and increased expenditures to fix deficiencies in prior work.

After consulting the homeowners' agreement, the board should be certain of what it is responsible for in regards to upkeep of the exterior of the buildings. The agreement will often make the board responsible for the paint or stain in order to maintain a uniform appearance but leave the homeowner responsible for the siding, trim and other decorative finishes, such as window shutters. The split responsibility does create extra work for the board and property manager, but it also provides a check on those boards who would needlessly saddle homeowners with extensive repair costs.

The first order of business is to determine the current condition of the paint and underlying siding (for our purposes, any wood material, such as cedar siding, shakes, etc., which can be painted or stained). Even though the property manager can do this preliminary inspection, it is important that the board members also walk the property and see with their own eyes (and hands) what they are up against. Is there peeling, bubbling or flaking paint? Has the stain faded unevenly? Is there mold or mildew on the surfaces? Are siding or shingles cracked? Are trim and fascia boards showing signs of rot? Has the wood previously been sanded down many times? Are some homes in much worse shape than others? Are all surfaces easily accessible for painting or are there shrubs and flowers in the way? Are attached wood decks to be painted or stained, and what is their condition? All of the above must be known in order for the board and management agency to develop a comprehensive plan to properly address all items of concern.

Paint Problems

Peeling paint is almost always a sign that water has been absorbed by the siding or insulation material and is preventing proper adhesion of the paint and primer to the wood surface. Surprisingly, even moisture from a kitchen or bathroom with an outside wall can seep through the insulation and eventually evaporate through the top surface of the siding. More likely, though, there is an entry point for rainwater, and the wood is being soaked on the inside. Frequently this can be traced back to poor caulking, siding installation, or cracked siding that has not been sealed. Water may also enter from the top if gutters and leaders, and possibly roofing are not properly installed, flashed and caulked. If this problem is seen on just a handful of homes, the problem is probably isolated. This does not mean determining the source of the problem will be any easier, but in most cases finding some difference between the majority good homes and the minority bad homes is possible.

Regardless, it is imperative that the origin of the problem be determined prior to other work being undertaken so that appropriate arrangements can be made to fix the issue before or in conjunction with the painting process. These repairs should be finished before the new paint is applied so that no further damage takes place. *It is imperative that any siding or trim that is replaced be properly primed.* Unfortunately, although many carpenters and painters will buy pre-primed wood, they fail to re-prime where cuts are made, thus allowing a point of entry for moisture into the wood.

Bubbling paint can be a sign of moisture in the wood which is trying to vent through the paint but can also be caused by paint which has been applied when the surface is too hot, either due to high ambient temperatures or direct sunlight on the surface. Though painters are usually careful not to paint wet surfaces, they can be less so when it comes to high temperatures. The property manager or painting committee should discuss best practices with the contractor if there is a chance buildings will be painted during a heat wave or in very strong sunlight.

Flaking or cracks in the paint can be caused by excess moisture, but there are other culprits to check too. If flaking is seen on a small number of trim or siding pieces, it is possible they were previously replaced and not primed before painting. The primer is essential for not only sealing the wood but to also provide for better adhesion with the top coat of paint. Other shortcuts taken in preparation or application to look out for: paint applied over a still wet primer or first coat of paint, low quality paint, application of paint during high temperatures and low humidity, applying oil-based paint over an existing latex painted surface. Small areas may be scraped or brushed and then resurfaced with fresh paint, but this limited approach is best used only in less visible areas as it is very difficult to get a finish that is uniform across the whole board. For best results, brush and sand the entire board before priming and repainting.

Stain Problems

Fading stain is an unavoidable problem and will vary greatly depending on the type of stain and the amount of exposure to the sun and elements. The prime difficulty with faded stain is lack of uniformity. On decks, fading can be more pronounced in some areas because of poor application techniques or heavy traffic. Fading may be very pronounced on siding which is in direct sunlight, such as a southern exposure, but may be non-uniform because of shade from trees or other buildings.

There are only two approaches to re-staining in this situation. If the original stain is semi-solid, it will be necessary to remove the prior coat of stain to achieve a uniform reapplication. Trying to apply more stain over the heavily faded areas will not achieve an acceptable result. In the case of siding, if an entire side of the home is uniformly more faded than the rest, it may be possible to do an additional coat on that side to achieve a good overall presentation.

The other option is to refinish with a solid stain. However, solid stains come with their own issues, and the board should consider all ramifications of this choice. Solid stains are more paint-like and will be subject to flaking or peeling (especially when used on decks that receive heavy foot traffic), and the contrast from any exposed wood may be very noticeable. This is also a no "do over" option as it is virtually impossible to strip and remove all signs of the solid stain so that a semi-solid can be reapplied. However, when wood is very aged, this may be the least worst option open to the board.

The board must also consider whether to use an oil- or latex-based stain. A latex-based stain can be applied over a previously applied oil-based stain if an oil-based primer is used first. Do not apply an oil-based stain over an older latex-based finish; it will never dry properly. Proponents of latex-based solutions note that oil-based stains are more prone to mold or mildew. This is because the latex products add mildicides to reduce the chance of mildew growth. Oil-based proponents will point out that these mildicides may lose their effectiveness quite quickly and that ultimately, all surfaces will need a periodic light power wash to keep mold and mildew at bay. Too, oil-based stains usually will weather better than their latex counterparts. When in doubt, stick with the same type of stain as used previously.

Surface Preparation and Siding

Mold and mildew on the wood surfaces *must be completely removed* prior to any additional preparation work and eventual repainting. The best practice is to promptly clean the surfaces at the first sign of mold and mildew with a light power wash, but often corners are cut in the name of saving money that lead to recurring problems. Once mold and mildew take over, they are very difficult to be rid of as they live off of the paint. A good painting contractor will recommend a light, *low pressure* power wash prior to sanding and other preparatory work and if there is mildew, a mildicide should be added to the solution.

If the mold and mildew are severe, then hand brushing may be required in addition to the wash down. A high pressure wash should be used as a last resort since it can cause permanent damage to the wood surface. The property manager needs to review all cleaning plans with the contractor prior to the start of the work to make sure all surfaces are cleaned – including leaders and gutters, shutters, etc. Plans should also be in place to protect any nearby shrubs and spray them with clean water when finished.

Even though sanding down to the wood surface may reduce future mildew, it is both costly and impractical. Furthermore, it can result in other problems if not done correctly, i.e., swirls in the surface if rotary sanders are used improperly or poor paint adhesion if the surface is made too smooth. After consultation with the painting contractor, if there remain concerns that mold and mildew will return, a mildicide should be added to the primer and possibly the paint itself. Doing so may reduce the lifetime of the paint finish but it will still be longer than if no treatment were added at all.

Siding boards will crack over time, either of natural or water-related causes. Though small cracks (three or four inches) can be sealed, any boards with long cracks should be replaced. Unfortunately, it is often difficult to only replace one row of siding. To gain access to the bad row it is common to remove the row directly above, and depending on how cleanly the siding comes off, that second row may not be suitable for reuse. Often a long crack will be only a fraction of the total length of a piece of siding. *To save money, this bad segment may be cut out but ensure that procedures are in place that require a certain minimum length of uncut board to remain to avoid creating a patchwork look.* A good minimum length to require is four to six feet.

Rotted siding or trim are signs of water damage or possibly termite activity. If water is the cause, the source should be found and measures taken to prevent a recurrence. Like cracked siding, rotted trim should be removed and a certain minimum length be required when only removing a bad segment. Trim can be made of pine, cedar or other woods as well as synthetics, such as Azek ®. Where possible, pine should be avoided as it has a shorter lifetime, and the cost differential between pine and a better wood is insignificant when compared to the cost of the labor to make the repairs. Azek ® can last forever but does carry a few burdens: it is usually significantly more expensive than any wood alternative and can be difficult to use when replacing a segment of trim as Azek ® is very uniform while wood is not (seams may be more apparent to the eye). Azek ® is a good alternative if only a limited amount of material needs to be replaced and entire lengths can be removed to avoid the segmentation issue.

An older development may have been through many painting cycles with siding and trim subject to extensive sanding. As noted earlier, sanding is necessary to the proper preparation of the surface to be painted but it is not without downsides. Sanders can embed marks and gouges into the wood surface which will be visible under certain lighting conditions. An exceptionally smooth siding will not allow paint to adhere as well as one with a slightly rough surface. When evaluating the pre-existing condition of the buildings to be painted, care should be taken to determine if the above problems are present and, if so, whether they are extensive enough to consider replacing the affected siding and trim. The decision will need to strike a balance between costs to both the association and homeowners, appearances and the probability of future paint adhesion problems.

Other Preparations

An often overlooked element of a painting project is the location and types of plants, shrubs and trees near the homes. Painters must have room to work but tying back shrubs that are in the way may cause them severe damage, if they can be tied at all. Flowers may be trampled. In addition, any plants that are too close to the home increase moisture on and near the painted surfaces which can lead to or accelerate the growth of mold and mildew. Trees which have limbs overhanging the homes can result in significant clogging of gutters with flowers, seeds and leaves which then leads to overflows and water damage to the siding and paint.

Thus the board must develop certain standards to be followed by the homeowners and landscaper regarding the proximity of plantings to the homes. A bare minimum separation is 12" with 24" to 36" to be preferred. If no attention has been paid to this need in prior years, getting compliance may be difficult as pruning or trimming may no longer be viable solutions. The board should consider having the association move plants and shrubs if homeowners are unable to do so on their own. This will be especially true if the homeowner has invested a large sum of money for plantings when no prior regulations specifying a minimum separation from the home existed.

Decks

Many homes have some kind of patio, deck or balcony. Unless specifically addressed in the homeowners' agreement, patio maintenance is a homeowner responsibility and rarely a concern of the association as this area is usually not easily seen by other homeowners or guests. One exception is when the association cuts or otherwise damages the patio in the context of repairing an item, which is its responsibility, such as repairing a drain pipe. In that case the association must return the area to its original state or arrange equivalent compensation to the homeowner.

However, wooden decks and balconies present an additional potential responsibility for the association. If the decks have been previously painted or stained by the association, then the association must assume responsibility for future maintenance of the paint or stain. In effect, the deck has become an extension of the siding and trim of the home. Repairs or replacement of the wood itself may remain a homeowner responsibility with similar guidelines as exist for siding and trim, but the preparation and painting will be at the association's cost. At first blush this might not seem to be a big deal except that decks and balconies can remain physically viable far longer than they may remain aesthetically viable.

As many developments are built with less than top-line materials, pressure- treated lumber is commonly found on decks and balconies. This wood can fulfill its structural mission for a very long time, measured in decades not years. But as the wood ages, it becomes more and more difficult to maintain an attractive finish with paints and stains. Small and large cracks in the wood grow over time, leading to cracked and chipped finishes. Normal activity on the deck, which once had no effect, will now quickly strip paint and stain. And as the wood ages, light stains will no longer look the same when applied, often resulting in a gradual shift to darker stains.

Unfortunately, just as with a paint, when darker colors flake, the damage is much more apparent against the exposed lighter wood surface below. This will no doubt result in complaints from the homeowners that their decks look terrible and to please re-stain (or paint) them now! When a deck is new, stains and paints will usually last up to three years before requiring remedial attention. Low use and sheltered balconies may last even longer. But as the wood ages from weather and usage, the good lifetime of a new finish may be reduced to only one year.

Thus the board must assess the condition of the decks and balconies and if they are to be repainted or stained, to properly manage homeowner expectations of the lifetime of the work as well as the appearance as it ages. A reasonable tact to take is to continue to use a light stain which is not a significantly different color than the aged bare wood. Though not likely to look as good as when applied to pristine wood, it will make chips and flakes less noticeable than a darker stain or paint.

Based on the above discussion, the board should avoid taking responsibility for painting and staining of decks if at all possible. If there is no precedent or homeowners' agreement requirement, simply establish guidelines for what are acceptable finishes for homeowners to use. If the board is stuck with a "pre-existing condition" created by a prior board, revert to as neutral a paint or stain as possible. Besides reduced complaints about chips and flakes, this will make it easier for homeowners to replace their old wood decks using new synthetic materials with a minimum of color conformity problems. However, this switch may be very difficult if a dark color was used as it will be nearly impossible to sand or chemically remove all traces of the old finish (not to mention financially costly).

An important take away from the pitfalls of decks and balconies is that the board must take care when selecting paint or stain colors for the sidings and trims. One can always go darker, but going significantly lighter may be impossible without significant sanding and many coats and thus practically impossible. For this reason, think long and hard before selecting a color much darker than the current surface – the board is potentially committing the association to this color, or a narrow variation, for decades to come.

Putting It All Together: A Painting Project

Appendix C is a process outline encompassing an entire painting project, from start to finish. Pay close attention to the remedial work that homeowners must perform; timely notification to the homeowners throughout the process is essential if the project is to be completed on schedule and without major incident. By communicating with the homeowners at all stages, they will know exactly what is expected of them and when.

Timelines, as also shown in Appendix C, should be developed by the board members most closely tied to the painting project in conjunction with the property manager and the contractor who will perform the work. Weather is a variable that is impossible to schedule directly, and for this reasons dates are viewed as targets and not absolutes. However, if the conclusion of a project could run into the start of cold weather, allowances must be built into the time line to account for rain and other delays.

Grounds

THE GROUNDS OF THE ASSOCIATION COMPRISE the entirety of the property as described in the homeowners' agreement and bylaws. Though certain portions of the property may be legally deeded to each homeowner, the association in almost all cases will have control over the care of the property, barring some narrowly defined exceptions. Landscaping the property is far more than "mow and blow" and it should not surprise the board that the cost of maintaining the grounds is the largest recurring, non-capital expense of the association.

It is important for board members to take a step back and consider the condition of the grounds from a resident's perspective. Foremost, does the property look nice? When driving into the complex, do board members think to themselves "Gee, I wish they could … " or "Are they ever going to …?" Are the grass areas primarily grass and not clover or other weeds? Are leaves, twigs and dirt left behind by the landscaping crew? Do lawns have patchy, burnt-out areas? Are shrubs misshaped or overgrown?

The overall appearance and financial cost of maintaining the property are the board's responsibility. The property manager is expected to maintain close contact with the landscaper and handle routine matters with general guidance from the board. If a board member will be fulfilling that role, there are a few pointers on how to speak to and arrange work with the landscaping crew at the end of this section.

Private Areas Around Homes

Ideally, the homeowners' agreement speaks to the areas of the deeded property that homeowners may landscape on their own. This is not always the case, and there may be conflicting or incomplete statements in each of or between the homeowners' agreement and the association's bylaws. Short of changing or modifying the appropriate sections to provide clarity, the board will need to do its best to interpret the original intent and clarify as necessary through rules and regulations. That said, many associations allow the homeowners to choose and plant the shrubs and flowers in the immediate vicinity of their home. The front of the homes, which are visible to visitors as well as other homeowners, may have (more) constraints on selections; patio and deck areas usually receive wider latitude.

What is natural and attractive for one area of the country may be very out of place in another. Yet most homeowners will of their own volition follow local customs, and for this reason, the board should not concern themselves with a list of allowed or approved flowers and shrubs – focus instead on those types that are clearly not acceptable. For example, there should be no vegetable or grain plantings in the front of the home (but perhaps some types are allowed on rear patios); climbing vines are best discouraged or severely limited to very slow growers; and large grasses may leave bare areas or unattractive foliage in the off season and are best reserved for common area use.

Whatever the board decides should be incorporated into the association's rules and regulations that are distributed periodically to all homeowners and residents. Changes to the policy should be sent with a regular mailing and posted with other board related notices. Be as clear as possible to reduce the chances of misunderstandings and unnecessary conflict with homeowners years later.

Most associations will also arrange for periodic pruning of all shrubs on common ground and will handle those of the homeowners at the same time. This avoids creating a scraggly look where some homeowners have pruned and others have not – and may never. This does not preclude homeowners from handling their own pruning or leaving special instructions for the landscapers. The property manager should announce the pruning schedule at least a week prior to its expected start and ask any homeowners who have special needs to contact the management agency with their requests. If the homeowner plans to handle the pruning themselves, the property manager should provide a hard cutoff date after which time the association will do the work (usually to coincide with the completion of pruning on the property).

Though already noted that the rear area of homes are generally given much more freedom, common sense rules do apply. If a homeowner's property extends 20, 30, 50 or more feet from the back entrance or patio edge, is it acceptable for them to till the ground and begin growing corn? Probably not. But many homeowners do wish to grow vegetables during the summer so it is essential that there be guidelines in place on what is permitted to grow on the patio or deck proper and what is or is not alright in the ground beyond.

If the board finds itself in a situation where a seasonal vegetable garden has been planted absent any regulations, do not create a confrontation. Instead, formally approve the new guidelines, provide a copy to the homeowners and inform the offending homeowner(s) that next season they must comply with these rules but a waiver is granted this year. The growing season is simply too short to merit engaging in an acrimonious back and forth over removal of plants on which a homeowner has spent money, time and personal effort.

The board should also be clear in its rules and regulations that plantings that are on common ground, no matter how beautiful, may be removed. Homeowners should always be required to consult the board, through the property manager, with any suggestions for plantings in common areas which they believe would improve the look of the property. In many cases, the board will agree to the suggestion so long as the homeowner provides the material and labor for the initial planting and that the required upkeep will not be excessive or create other issues, such as needing additional irrigation to survive. The board should try to be receptive to such offers but must also keep in mind that although owners come and go, maintenance will always fall on the association.

Trees

What about trees? Tree care will be covered at length below but in regards to the homeowners, no trees should be planted, pruned or removed without the written consent of the board or property manager. This is primarily for three reasons: the association is nearly always responsible for pruning, conformity with the general appearance of the property and long term suitability for the location in question. With regards to conformity, if the trees on the property are all conifers, it would not look right to drop a maple or other deciduous tree in front of a home. If most trees are tall, replacements or additions should also ultimately grow to be tall trees. Similarly, if the trees in front of homes are dogwood, the board would not want to break the look with some other type of tree even if it is of similar size.

The suitability of any tree may depend more on where it is to be located than upon the tree itself. A tree with physically large roots or a shallow root system should not be planted in the vicinity of sidewalks, curbs or the street. Poplar trees are banned in some municipalities from sidewalks as their shallow roots lift concrete slabs and break asphalt. Frontage between the home and street must be considered when selecting a tree. Maples are fairly fast growers and tend to cover a significant area with their limbs. They are not a good choice if there is only ten feet between the home and street as eventually branches will hit windows and extend over parking spaces. A mighty oak tree should only be planted on common ground and with a significant area over which it can tower unimpeded.

Two types of trees must be avoided no matter how beautiful the foliage or shape: trees that drop fruit or acorns. Berries are an obvious nuisance which not only can discolor sidewalks, but be tracked into homes and cars and permanently soil valuable carpeting. Berries in sufficient number can also create a slip hazard. Less obvious are the larger fruit trees, such as varieties of apple. Who will be responsible for picking up the large fruit as it falls to the ground? If left to rot, the fruit will be unsightly and attract bees. Homeowners do not like bees! Trees with acorns should also be avoided. Like the fruit trees, they will create a clean-up problem and potential slip hazard but have the additional potential to damage car hoods and to fill up gutters.

The association should arrange for an arborist to examine all of the trees on the property at least once per year and ideally twice, once in the late spring and again in late fall. The spring visit is important as this is when various infestations of bugs and fungus begin to show. In some cases treatment may be time critical – a difference of just a week can result in the loss of one or more trees. The arborist will be familiar with diseases that are common to the trees prevalent in the association's geographic area. If hazardous chemicals are used, have the property manager make sure that the appropriate signage is put up so that residents will avoid contact with the affected areas.

During the late fall, the arborist should be asked to develop a prioritized plan for pruning the trees on the property. Hazard and health are the top concerns; far below is appearance. Beyond the obvious consideration of suspect trees or limbs near a home, also look for problems over sidewalks and roads around the perimeter of the property. If tree limbs are near electric utility wires and not of dire immediate concern, the arborist or property manager may be able to contact the utility company to have those limbs trimmed as part of their regular pruning program. This can save the association hundreds and potentially thousands of dollars.

If, in consultation with the arborist and property manager, the board decides to remove a tree, further consideration should be given to the stump and any replacement planting. Stump grinding is expensive and should be skipped except in those areas where a stump could be a trip hazard or the unsightly remains would be undesirable.

When debating the replacement of a removed tree, the first point to look at is whether there truly is a need for a replacement. If the tree is one of many in a small area, then there is no need to absorb the cost. If it is a tree in front of a home, the homeowner will probably (though not always) want a replacement. Consideration should then focus on what is a suitable tree for that location on the property.

If the property is an older one, a unique situation may arise. Decades ago it was not unheard of to fill cavities in tree trunks with concrete, and often it is not obvious this has been done until a saw breaks! Depending on the extent of the fill, the board may face a choice of leaving a very tall stump (think five or more feet) or trying to pull out the remains of the tree by the roots using chains and heavy equipment.

Once the property manager has the prioritized work list and estimated costs from the arborist, the board should consider the proposal and remove any work which is deemed superfluous. The property manager should request the arborist quote for the work to be done during the winter months at discounted winter rates, if those are available.

Ideally, the board will have already established a budget for annual tree work and the estimate received will be within that cost. But if there is no budget or the estimate exceeds the remaining annual budget, the board will need to decide whether to make the entire expenditure or delay some of the work into the next budget year. Dangerous trees should always be addressed first due to the potential liability risk.

If the association is in a colder climate and has an unused area available, it may be possible to keep the majority of any downed trees for use as firewood by homeowners. From a financial standpoint, look to balance the cost of cutting and moving the wood to the storage location against the cost of chipping and eventual dumping by the arborist. No wood should ever be stored in close proximity to any buildings due to the increased risk of termite infestations.

Shrub Care

Pruning of shrubs will be done by the association's landscaper at least once and preferably twice a year. The first pruning takes place after the spring growth has begun to mature. Plants should be cut and shaped as appropriate for each species. If the flowering shrubs never flower and others seem to be just green tips and dead wood inside, the landscaping crew is probably doing a hatchet job with electric clippers.

The property manager will need to address that issue with the head landscaper. Flower buds should never be cut off and many shrubs require specific procedures to be sure the pruning creates not just a beautiful shrub but one which will continue to be so as it grows and ages. Once overgrown and improperly pruned, it is almost impossible to cut a bush back to the appropriate size without creating a leafless husk and thus having to expend funds for replacements. A landscaper who is unable to identify the plantings and prune them properly should be dismissed.

It is inevitable that at some point the shrubs and trees will be attacked by a parasite. Mites, scale, fungus, borers and many other ailments are common, though certainly unwelcome, as they may not only kill valued plants but also remove dollars from the association's bank accounts to pay for spraying and other treatments. Board members should always keep an eye out for changes in the appearance of trees and shrubs and inform the property manager promptly. The board should also encourage the homeowners to do the same.

Certain borers require near immediate treatment to prevent a tree from dying – think days to a few weeks – and can rapidly spread to other similar trees on the property. Scales can make quick work of shrubs too. The property manager should engage the association's arborist for both treatment of the immediate problem as well as development of future inoculation plans.

Flowers

There may also be varying amounts of floral arrangements in the common areas, in particular at the entrance to the community. The association's landscape contract should provide for a certain number of man hours to plant flowers and also to weed, mulch and otherwise maintain the flower beds (Mulching should be done in late spring and include common area shrubbery as well.) Even though the association may have an active garden (grounds) committee, over the long term membership enthusiasm and competence cannot be relied upon to plant flowers and maintain beds.

There should not be any difficulty, however, adjusting the landscaper's responsibilities to reflect the capabilities of the homeowner committee. The property manager should arrange a meeting between the committee and landscaper to establish appropriate boundaries and parameters to prevent misdirection of the landscaper while still ensuring they provide the services (or equivalent) in the association's contract. The board and property manager must make it clear to the landscaper that their goal is to have an amicable working relationship between the committee and landscaper, but it is the landscaper's responsibility to alert the property manager if there are difficulties.

With regard to flower selection, many associations will allow the landscaper to chose from what is readily available locally and thought to fit the look of the property. Others will, on their own or via a grounds committee, select certain flowers that the landscaper will procure and then plant. In a minority of cases, the grounds committee may have avid and competent gardeners who the board trusts to make these selections. In the latter case, procurement should be handled by the property manager (possibly in conjunction with the landscaper) so as to stay within the annual flower budget. This method also avoids the need for homeowners to provide receipts and wait for reimbursement checks.

Landscapers will almost always choose annual type flowers as this ensures them of a markup each year on new plants. Annuals are generally more colorful than perennials and are well-known to homeowners. Two common examples are impatiens and begonias. However, from a financial standpoint, it is to the association's advantage to make the majority of the common area flowers perennials. The initial cost of the plants are comparable but the perennials will grow for many, many years if taken care of properly. A changeover from all annuals to perennials will take from four to five years to complete. Even though the time frame is long, much of the new planting will be done in the first two years. Years three through five will see the new plants divide and spread out to completely fill in the selected areas.

In this regard, some patience will be required by both the board and homeowners as beds may appear thin during those first few years. Annuals should not be banished entirely as they can be used to fill in areas when the perennials are thin and also as borders. A limited number of annual beds can also be kept to allow for variety and in some cases may be more appropriate given lighting, soil and irrigation considerations. The board must take care that flowers (and shrubs) do not obstruct the ability of drivers to see other vehicles and pedestrians – sunflowers and certain types of grasses are poor choices near corners and mailboxes.

It is important that the flowers and plants selected be reviewed by the board and property manager not just for aesthetics, but also with an eye toward maintenance. Flowers selected should not require an undue amount of dead heading (removal of old blooms) or annual thinning. Far more important though are water requirements. Some plants, such as hydrangea, will require significant water throughout the season and especially the first few years as roots are established. If the property does not have in-ground irrigation lines which will provide this water, the board is better off selecting a more drought tolerant plant. Although homeowners may promise to water from their own hoses or buckets, they will not promise to repay the association for dead plants if they fail to remember to do so.

However, one alternative in climates that do receive some degree of rainfall is to install plastic rain barrels near those flower beds and plants. Pricing is reasonable and the containers are designed to minimize the chance they are used as a breeding ground by flying insects. Helpful homeowners are then more likely to assist in the watering as they will not have to drag their own hoses (or multiple hoses) to the plants. At the worst, the landscaper can now be asked to water during the weekly visit.

Lawns

Lawn care is by far the largest part of any landscaper's job with weekly work required from at least late April through late October. It is essential that the property manager know the landscaper's plans for the application of fertilizer, pre-emergent and other chemical treatments for the grass. Look closely at the landscaping contract to determine which of these services are included and which are to be billed as additional items. In particular, be aware that some landscapers will subcontract out the chemical treatments. If the contract includes such work, do not let the landscaper try to submit subcontractor bills for reimbursement! The property manager should review the scheduling of treatments to make sure they are put down at the proper time of year, adjusting for any unusual weather trends, and further, to make sure that the work is actually done.

Whenever chemicals or fertilizers are used, the board must require the landscaping crew to put signage in the affected areas. The property manager can also put up notices on bulletin boards or mailbox structures. Homeowners with small children or pets become extremely irate when not warned to avoid the treated areas and for how long.

Over time, the ground will settle and run-off water from the homes will contribute to changes in the ability to maintain grass in those areas. The board should be on the lookout for swampy areas where water is pooling. Besides creating a muddy mess and increasing the chances of grass-killing disease, mosquitoes and other bugs will use the area to breed. At best, this will create a nuisance; at worst it can spread Eastern equine encephalitis or West Nile virus. The board should alert the management agency to these problem areas if the property manager has not already brought them to their attention. For minor problems the landscaper may be able to alter the soil composition to provide better drainage qualities. Bigger water problems may require the installation of a French drain or other in-ground assistance to move water into storm basins or retention ponds.

Many landscapers try to be jack-of-all-trades; in addition to regular grounds work they will also do drainage work, wall building and paving. Doing such one stop shopping may sound attractive (and it certainly is less work for the property manager), but a specialist may give equal or better service at lower cost, while avoiding the downsides of making the property a gold mine for the landscaper. This is not to say never give these other types of jobs to the landscaper, rather the board should fully consider alternative vendors and ask for competitive bids. Establishing working relationships with specialized contractors on midsized jobs may also be of benefit when emergencies or larger jobs emerge for which the board cannot rely on the abilities of the landscaper.

How the landscaper cuts the grass can also play a part in how well the lawns look in the summer months. Even though optimum heights will vary depending on the primary type, all grasses will look nicer if cut a bit taller in the peak summer months so as to better hold any available moisture. Don't push this too far though lest the lawns look unkempt and other problems develop.

Attention to the small details, such as mower height, can make a big difference in the attractiveness of the property. Although most landscapers are quite handy with the weed whacker, they may not be quite as handy with a hoe and thus let the edging around shrubs and flower beds fill in. The landscape crew should also remove or otherwise keep in check grass and weeds which can spring up in cracks in sidewalks and roadways. In an ideal world the property manager will look after such finer details, but the reality is the board members and other homeowners are best positioned to notice when things are let go.

Irrigation

Depending on the local climate and size of the property, in-ground irrigation may be another board responsibility and one that will intertwine with the landscaper's efforts. If natural rainfall alone is relied upon to water the lawns and plants, there is little the board can do to avoid lawn brownout during the summer months. Further, any efforts to help shrubs and new trees during time of drought by use of hose or buckets may be difficult, if not impossible. This is a mixed blessing for the board – the property may not always look its best but there is nothing which can be changed short of installing an irrigation system. Having an irrigation system, however, does not magically make all problems go away and in fact can create additional work for the board and property manager.

Irrigation systems are installed and maintained by special-ized contractors who only handle this kind of work. Prices and service can vary considerably; if the board is not happy with the current contractor they should not hesitate to ask the property manager to investigate other local firms. The size of the firm is not as important as their reputation – it does not matter how many trucks or techs are available if the results are poor.

Sometime during the spring, the irrigation company will run

system checks and perform maintenance prior to turning the system back on. Normally, each sprinkler head is checked to make sure it rises and falls properly and the aim is correct. Note that the board will always receive complaints from homeowners about water being misdirected. Though this may be because the landscapers have inadvertently changed the direction of a head, many times it is because the irrigation tech was faced with a no-win situation and had to strike the best balance between minimizing water contact with structures or personal property and actually watering the surrounding areas.

The techs will also check that there are no apparent leaks from broken conduits and that rain gauges are still functional. If the association does not have rain gauges installed, they should consider doing so. Though not infallible and perhaps more delicate than ideal, rain gauges will save the association money over the long run by reducing water usage. Gauges also minimize the effects of overwatering resulting in bugs and swampy areas. Finally, the technicians will set an initial watering program into the control hardware that is appropriate for the season. To save on service calls, the property manager and a board member should be familiar with the control units so that watering cycles can be adjusted seasonally and during times of drought or flood. Remember, too, that the association is not exempt from local and statewide water restrictions during time of drought.

Lawns are best watered between midnight and 5 A.M. Watering during the daytime and early evening should be avoided to prevent burning and possible mold and fungus problems. Even a midsized property may have multiple control units thus a map or other notational record should be made to associate control units and stations with actual physical locations on the property. Be aware that multiple control units may be served from the same water source and thus care must be taken to be certain adequate water pressure is maintained. If not, the sprinkler heads may not rise or water spray the required distances. When the units cannot be operated simultaneously, schedule one to begin after the other completes rather than using alternating days. This avoids complications during dry spells when it may be necessary to increase the frequency of watering. For a similar reason, there should be a gap between the finish of one control unit's cycle and the start of another to allow for the extension of the duration of watering at each station.

Most modern control units allow specific times to be set for each station, thus areas with flowers can be left on longer and naturally damp areas can be shorter. The entire process of adjusting the days and durations of stations is quite easy and there is no reason why the association should pay service calls to the irrigation company when the property manager can make changes during a regular weekly visit, or in a pinch, by one of the board members.

Fall Foliage

Associations in climates with complete seasonality will also have the pleasure of fall foliage ... and its aftermath. Every crew is capable of handling leaf removal, but the board should be sure that shortcuts are not taken, such as purposely blowing excess leaves into shrubs or against remote fences. The landscaper should be required to also blow out ground level patio areas as well as pool decks and tennis courts. Municipalities vary as to restrictions on the use and type of leaf blowers; the board should not ask for scheduling changes which might result in fines for the landscaper or the association.

Pickup of leaves will also vary by municipality; some require bagging, others may allow leaves to be blown off the curb and onto the street. Still others may not make any arrangements for disposal, and it is left up to the property owner to follow whatever guidelines may be in place. Even though burning is a legal option in some areas of the country, it often is not and comes with its own set of risks. If the association must dispose

146 A FRAMEWORK FOR HOA MANAGEMENT

of the leaves on its own, consider setting up a composting system. This can range from the simple (a sheltered remote area of the property) to the complex (specially designed composting bins). Shredding of the leaves will, of course, reduce the volume they take up and will limit flyaway.

Snow Removal

For a large part of the country, the main wintertime concerns are snow, ice or both. Contracting for plowing either will be with an independent operator or with the current landscaper. Plow service can be flat rate or per storm, with salt and sand most often considered extra billable items. Pricing may be better with an independent contractor but be warned, there are hidden risks beyond how good a job they do.

For instance, a single or small operator may not be able to handle a season with frequent snow and will walk away from a flat rate contract. Although the board and homeowners may think they have a legally binding service contract, in reality it is nothing more than an agreement on pricing. A lawsuit is near certain to cost more than the contract, and it will not get the streets plowed and sidewalks shoveled during the next storm. Perhaps, instead, a per storm payment plan was chosen. The plow crew seems fine for the small storms but looks overwhelmed during a heavy snowfall. Depending where the association is in the pecking order, (i.e., how much is paid), it may not always see the roads plowed in a timely manner, if at all. Again, the association's recourse is for all intents limited to finding another operator.

On the other hand, a landscaper who also handles plowing is more likely to ensure they have sufficient equipment and manpower to handle typical winter conditions since the primary value of the the contract is for landscaping work done the rest of the year. It is in the landscaper's best interest not to let any failings at plowing derail an otherwise lucrative landscaping contract. However, this is not to say that the landscaper will prove themselves to be the best at plowing, just that they are less of a risk of complete failure to the association.

Many of the issues noted for an independent operator also apply to a landscaper. On a flat-fee contract in a season of frequent snow, the landscaper may be forced to limit the hours they plow so as to minimize overtime to the workers. Roads that were plowed during the night at the start of the season may not be taken care of at the end until daylight hours. Probably less of an issue are very heavy snowfalls. Though all customers will see some fall off in service simply as a result of the unusual demands placed on the plow crews, the landscaper is likely to work hard to get all clients taken care of to some degree.

The choice of a per storm or flat-fee contract is dependent upon location and will require a knowledge of not just the typical number of storms (snow or ice) but also how many are in the outlier years. If the board finds that it has little flexibility in the association's finances to handle a bad winter, the best choice will be a flat-fee contract, even if the normal winter only has a few events. The board must always think of and be prepared for worst cases; demanding an immediate special assessment to pay for continued snow removal is not a situation the board would wish to find itself. Of course, taking a large flat-fee contract and then seeing a season with few storms will also make the board feel dumb and may even prompt complaints from some homeowners. Keep in mind that over the long run, seasons average out, and in some years a flat-fee will be to the association's benefit and others it will enrich the landscaper.

The board should seek the pricing structure which best protects the association's finances *over the long term*. If the property is located in a part of the country where snow and ice are infrequent, then by all means select a per storm contract if there are reserves available to handle an unusual season. In an area that typically sees a lot of snow but maybe has not recently, do not gamble the association's finances on potential short term savings; take the flat-fee contract. The board may even be able to negotiate a hybrid contract that stipulates a per storm charge up to a certain number of storms and then is capped by a flat-fee for any and all additional storms or vice versa. Do not be caught up in cookie-cutter solutions that are easy for the property manager to arrange; request what the board believes to be an optimum arrangement for the association and let the agent bring back the proposals.

The salting and sanding of the property is a windfall to whomever is doing the work: these "consumables" are almost always off-contract and billed after each use. Of course, safety is a paramount concern, but it is a good idea to require approval from the property manager (when practicable) before putting down salt or sand. At the least, this establishes that there is no carte blanche and the operator should be judicious in deciding when salt and sand are used. Along with street plowing, the board will likely contract to have common area walkways and public sidewalks outside the property shoveled with salt and sand applied as necessary.

Many associations will have homeowner walks and drive-ways taken care of too, in part to reduce liability risk and in part to minimize the number of independent contractors on the property at any one time. It can quickly become a mess if multiple contractors and day laborers are all putting snow where they see fit. Containers with sand or a salt/sand mixture can be placed near mailboxes or other common areas to allow residents to touch up an area which has become icy from foot traffic. The same can also be used by residents and delivery trucks should they find they have become stuck and need extra traction on an icy roadway. A property with many pets can explore using pet-friendly salt on the sidewalks and elsewhere.

The property manager, in conjunction with the board, should establish guidelines for both the residents and snow-removal crews to follow during the winter. All on-site preparations need to be complete well before the first snowfall is expected. Except in very small developments, the plow crew should be instructed to rotate which area is cleared first so no group of homeowners feels they are forgotten or always last. Objects such as fire hydrants, decorative lighting, in-ground refuse containers and the like should all be marked with flexible stakes. This will reduce the chance of inadvertent damages during heavy snows and allow the crews to find those things that must be dug out after each storm. In particular, plow operators should know where in-ground electric and gas utility access points are so that they do not cover them with a five foot pile of snow.

Many associations already have difficult parking situations which can be made worse as snow accumulates and make subsequent snow removal even more difficult. The property manager should develop plans with the plow crew that establish specific locations for piling up the snow. If necessary, some parking spots may need to be reserved and specially marked to prohibit parking during and after snowstorms so the plow trucks can store the snow. These storage locations should be as near storm drains and away from homes as possible to prevent flooding when temperatures warm and the snow begins to melt. The board should also consider whether any excess snow will be front loaded and trucked off the property or if a location on-site with the necessary access is available to dump the excess snow.

Homeowners need to understand that snow removal is a process and that the fastest results will come with the least interaction with them and the plow crew. Homeowners should be advised not to move cars in the hope their parking space will be plowed quickly, and they certainly should not be asking shovelers to stop and remove snow from their cars while they are engaged in other work. The primary objectives are to clear the roadways, provide access to the parking areas and clear the sidewalks, in that order. Plowing open parking spots is a low priority and is usually taken care of only after all the other work is done – not only at the property but any others the operator must clear. In heavy or lengthy storms this may mean that clean up will take more than one day. By stopping the crews to ask for favors or individual attention, the residents are only slowing the entire process.

Resident safety is also very important. Along with other "winter rules" which the board will instruct the property manager to distribute, a stern warning not to walk behind plow trucks or in areas they are working should be at, or near the top of the list. Each year there are multiple tragic, fatal incidents of people struck by plow trucks or pets that were run over. These trucks have limited vision, particularly in the rear and operating in snowy conditions makes them far more dangerous to be near. Even pulling out of a parking space or driveway should be done very cautiously. Residents should be asked to contact the property manager promptly if their car or personal property is damaged during the snow removal and if possible, to provide photo documentation with time stamps. The property manager can then arrange for the snow removal company to provide monetary reimbursement or arrange for repairs.

Under certain conditions the board may find they need to be more lenient about the enforcement of some rules and regulations. As the winter snows accumulate, space comes at a premium. Parking spots may shrink or disappear, resulting in homeowners parking in guest spots. Garbage may need to be set out off the curb or more prominently lest it be lost in the snow and never removed. Completely picking up after pets becomes a challenge as droppings are lost in the snow: the board may wish to consider partially shoveling areas known to be frequented by pets to alleviate this problem. To mitigate ugly parking confrontations, the winter rules should include a reminder to always ask prior to "borrowing" another homeowner's parking spot, even when shifting cars to give better access to the plows for parking space cleanup.

There will be days when everyone, board members included, will need to take a deep breath and just let it go. In particular, do not obsess over minor damages. Lawns will often be damaged as plows push snow back off the road or into overflow storage locations. The ground can be re leveled and grass grown quickly in the spring so that any winter damage will be gone in short order. In fact, one of the primary reasons to consider having an overflow storage location on the property is that the cost to repair the grass is far less than the cost to truck snow off the property.

Landscaper Speak

Earlier it was noted that on smaller properties a board member may have significant oversight of the grounds. This may also be the case if the property has unique plants or simply that the board wishes to have tighter control over the appearance of the property.

Most landscaping operations are relatively small sole proprietorships and rarely have any significant corporate structure behind them. Often the business is a family affair with a spouse, cousin, etc helping with billing, supplies and even answering the phone. The area of operations typically cover the nearest two or three towns. Some of the larger landscapers may employee upwards of 50 laborers and may branch out to include light drainage and paving work. These secondary fields enable one stop shopping for their customers, and the service provided is probably adequate for smaller jobs. This type of landscaper may also be able to provide services on very short notice.

Understand that the landscaper is not FedEx or IBM. The phone may sometimes go unanswered and transfer to voice mail. The detail and presentation of bills will be sufficient but not necessarily reflective of a top-notch computer or accounting department. Unless the bills and the information in them are completely wrong, there is little to be gained by complaining about presentation as the landscaper will not have the resources to make changes (though a suggestion for the future may be appreciated). "Timely" response may range from a few hours to a day or two depending upon the request. Many individuals working in high pressure jobs in major cities operate at a significantly different speed than the landscaper, and this can cause friction if expectations are not tempered.

When speaking with the landscaper it is best to keep things simple and to the point, trying to be as specific as possible. Speaking in generalities is likely to lead to trouble and misunderstanding. Do not ask the landscaper to "put in some flowers around the rotary," ask them to "Put some red and pink impatiens and red begonias around the rotary. If those available do not look healthy, call and let me know what does look in good shape."

This is not to say that the landscaper has no knowledge of plants. Many do, though their expertise in picking the right plant for the right location may vary considerably. For instance, if grass refuses to grow in a certain area, ask for the two best alternatives in their opinion, including the cost and water requirements, and use that information to make a selection.

Lawn care should be a line item discussion: when are you putting pre-emergent down, when are you putting fertilizer down, raise the mower height on June 21, etc. Do not just ask "How's the grass doing?" Let the landscaper know that the board is aware of all contractual obligations and they expect timely fulfillment.

When meeting with the landscaper on the property, do not have a list of items so long that the landscaper is likely to forget the important points or tasks because they do not have an administrative assistant with them. If the board member is working from a printed list, they should extend the courtesy to the landscaper and give them a copy to add notes on and take with them.

Following the above advice to keep things simple and direct, and treating the landscaper professionally and with respect, should go far in ensuring a successful relationship.

Miscellaneous

THERE ARE A NUMBER OF MISCELLANEOUS ITEMS the board has responsibility for that do not fall neatly into the facilities, structures or grounds categories. Some are minor but a few can carry significant risk and cost for the association.

Electric Meter Pans

Outside of the home are usually electric, gas and possibly water meters. Of concern to the board are electric "meter pans." A meter pan is a metal box affixed to the side of the home into which the live circuity is hooked first into the electric company's metering device and then to the wiring from the home. Over time these meter pans will rot out, often from the bottom up, potentially exposing children, landscapers and other workers to severe electric shock or possible death. Moreover, short circuits can be created back to the main junction which feeds homes on that section of the street. In the worst case, a fire could develop. For this reason, the association has multiple legitimate interests in ensuring that the pans are in a safe condition.

Unfortunately, even though common sense might dictate meter pans are the property of the electric company, they are in fact the sole responsibility of the homeowner. The property manager should do an annual inspection, and notify any homeowners with deficient meter pans they need to be replaced by a certain date or face fines or charge backs if the association must do the change out. Any qualified electrician will be able to handle this, and the board should recommend that in conjunction with a meter pan replacement that the owner have the home's electrical grounding checked. Do not take for granted that any homes, row town homes in particular, were properly grounded when built or that the proper gauge wiring was used. Homeowners may find that sporadic electrical problems that have troubled them for years are traced back to poor or non-existent grounding.

Patching and Paving

There are many forces that conspire against asphalt, such as weather and utility companies, and the board would do well to reserve some funds in the budget to cover regular, minor repair work. Eventually, plans will need to expand to encompass a complete repavement.

Potholes are an annual problem for any association in a northern climate with roadways more than five years old. During the winter, any significant potholes which develop can be cold patched on a temporary basis to minimize damage to cars and risk to pedestrians. In early spring, the property manager should survey all paved areas for winter damage from frost heaves, flooding, pot holes and general wear and tear. Asphalt production only occurs during warm weather months and most plants re-open by late April or early May. By that time, the board should be given a prioritized list of remedial work that needs to be done and the property manager's personal cost estimate for each type of repair. If the repair costs are expected to exceed what has been budgeted, the board will need to determine if all the work is critical and fund any excess through the general reserve account.

For small jobs, such as pothole repair, the property manager will arrange with a contractor to do the work on a day he has left over asphalt from a larger job. This makes the best economic sense for all parties involved. For slightly larger jobs, such as repavement of a section of roadway that has delaminated or repair of a caved in parking spot, the board should solicit proposals from two, and perhaps three, contractors. The property manager may recommend a bid from the company who does the association's drain work as they are equipped to handle smaller paving repairs as part of their primary work. Larger landscaping companies may also do paving or masonry work as a side business. Do not expect to get a good price from a large contractor who only does road paving – they may return a bid as a courtesy but the job is likely to be too small to be worth their time and effort.

Before soliciting bids, the board should ascertain if the damages were the result of utility company work. For example, if a water pipe breaks and the pavement around it collapses, the property manager should be able to have the water company do the repair at their own cost by their own employees or subcontractor. More generally, in the case of water damage, if there is still water in the area the water company will test the water for chlorination and may use audio devices to pinpoint the source of any leak. Electric, gas and cable companies may sometimes dig up a parking space to reach pipes or conduits. If that particular area later suffers a collapse or other failure, the property manager may be able to go back to the utility that did the work to request they make repairs. More difficult, however, will be getting a utility to repair work to adjoining areas long after the fact. Unfortunately, not every utility crew will take the time and effort to properly fill and compact the dirt where they have dug, especially if the utility uses a subcontractor to do the final fill and patch work. The result is seeming mysterious pavement collapses many months or years later as the soil shifts and settles.

The board may also desire to periodically treat the asphalt with a thin sealer coat to extend the life of the pavement as well as to give a fresh look to the roads and parking areas. This type of work is always followed by the repainting of traffic indicators and parking space lines, and often a firm that does line painting will also do seals. Unlike a private homeowner who may seal their 20' driveway annually, quickly and at minimal cost, logistics and the cumulative cost will restrict how often the typical HOA will preform this kind of maintenance.

Parking Areas and Road Markings

Generally speaking, parking lots are a low maintenance item for the board. The lines that mark the parking spaces, parking restrictions or traffic flow need to be resprayed periodically depending on the climate, road surface and usage. White paint should be used except when marking off larger no parking or restricted areas with cross hatching, in which case yellow should be used. Small sections of the curb near fire hydrants may also be marked in red.

There are likely to be a number of independent contractors who do this type of work, and many of the larger paving companies may also provide this service separate from paving services. When asking for estimates, do not be shocked to see a wide range of prices. The property manager may already have a list of contractors they have dealt with on other projects, but the board should also check with their local department of public works to see who is handling the line painting on their local roads. Many would be surprised to know that in smaller towns and cities (even near large metropolitan areas) this type of work may be done by a two or three man outfit, some who may even be part-time DPW employees. Their price is often lower than and work comparable to higher priced contractors.

Before going to proposal, the board should determine if any existing markings on the roads will be modified or if new ones are to be added. Often the board will find that safety will be improved if traffic flows only in one direction around a court yard or island within the parking lot. Directional arrows can then be added but before doing so, consider the amount of pushback expected and under what circumstances a homeowner can cut the arrow, if at all. Expect angry homeowners if suddenly the board requires them to drive all the way around a parking lot to park in their driveway when previously they could turn in immediately upon entering the parking area.

The board should show restraint and not go overboard with

roadway markings. Besides the negative aesthetics of too much paint on the roadways, if everything is marked "No!" people will simply ignore the markings. Be sure where "No Parking" is marked really is deserving of that notation for safety reasons. Often residents will find temporary parking in places not officially marked as such but which really do not interfere with other parking, traffic flow or emergency vehicles. Rather than mark it "No Parking" because it seems to be "unauthorized," consider marking a full space out of the location or perhaps one with a specific time limit to signify it is only for temporary use.

Use of reserved parking is tied to home ownership, and the homeowners' agreement may specify the number of designated parking space each home shall have. This may vary depending on the style of development and the model of the home when there is not uniformity. For instance, an attached townhouse may receive two reserved parking spaces in front of their home although the end unit, which has a garage and driveway, may only receive one designated space. Identify those spaces with whatever method was chosen to identify the homes in the development(letters, numerals or both). For illustration here, the designation is a numeral.

There are three methods to designating reserved parking spaces. Signage at the curb to indicate the ownership of the space is common, but is not always pretty (think small metal signs) and may still result in unauthorized parking. The goal should be to prevent even pulling into a reserved space unless authorized to do so. Signs can be difficult to see prior to pulling in, especially when the open space is between two large vehicles. Once a car pulls in, the chances of it backing out and continuing to search for a guest spot are not good. Lazy will usually win out over respectful! Signs are also subject to ongoing maintenance as the front end of vehicles may bend the sign posts, as will the plowing of snow over the curb.

Another technique is to paint the number on the vertical portion of the curb. Even though this is the least intrusive of the three methods, it suffers the same initial visibility problem as do signs but also may disappear entirely for long periods during the winter as snow is plowed against the curb. If used, make sure to have the number painted on a contrasting background to enhance visibility. Reflective paint will also help at night.

The third way is to paint the number on the pavement at the start of the space, if possible using a reflective paint. This is the most visible method (except during the time of snowfall) and should discourage all but the most lazy visitors from parking in a designated space as the word "guest" or "visitor" will standout prominently as cars drive along the lot. The downside is the increased amount of writing on the pavement, yet this can still be a better aesthetic choice than some signs, requires infrequent maintenance and does not interfere with landscaping. Which ever method the board decides to use, do make sure that the guest spaces are marked so as to leave no question in drivers minds of what is reserved and what is not.

The board should also review any requests to move designated (numbered) parking spaces. It is inevitable that each year a homeowner will ask to move a parking space because of some problem – damage from birds; damage from tree sap; the neighbors own two gigantic SUVs. The board, in considering the request, should look to see if a guest space may be exchanged to provide the accommodation without significant impact upon other residents. If there are an excess of guest parking spaces, it does no harm to swap the spot. However, if the board believes this will only open the floodgates to many more requests for identical reasons (a row of homes who all suffer from bird droppings), the board should deny the request.

Notification to homeowners should be made well in advance of the expected date of the line painting and any alternate rain dates. Additional notices should be put up one or two days prior in prominent locations, such as mail boxes or light poles. The property manager should include in the notification the details of how long the road and parking area will be closed and where residents should park in the interim. Except in a very small development, this will be a multiple day process as the number of cars that must be moved is significant and excess parking spaces limited.

Signage

The first thing any resident or guest sees when visiting the association is some kind of signage identifying the property. It is always a good idea to make a good first impression, and the board should periodically consider the state of the signage on the property from both physical and aesthetic standpoints. As well as the signage at the entrance, there may be street, directional and building signs scattered about the property. Like everything else, signs will show physical decay over time which can vary in rate and appearance depending on the material(s) used in their construction and the local climate. Metal can rust; wood can split, get termites or mold; plastics can fade from time in the sun and foams can chip. What was once a good looking sign may instead bring back not so fond memories of the 1980s or 1990s.

If the board does decide to explore replacing the signs, they will need to keep other important points in mind. Though the chosen material and intricacy of the design will factor into the cost, expect to pay between $5,000 and $10,000 for a pair of well made entrance signs, including installation. Unless the property entrance is on a dead end with no cross street, a pair of signs is required for best visibility from passing cars.

When considering the various styles available, thought must also be given to how it will be mounted. Will it be on a fence? Stand alone posts? Hanging? How is the visibility affected by the surroundings? If a sign is placed on top of a fence, it may be lost in the background during the day time. Any sign may become less visible if the wrong colors are used – for instance choosing a green sign and mounting it against a background of green grass. Although a hanging sign may look attractive (and only one required if lettering is on both sides), it may be unpractical if it is not large enough or in bright enough colors to be easily read at a distance from a car driving 30 mph. From a visibility standpoint alone, the safe choice is to place the sign against a solid fence or stone wall with a contrasting background at a height of four to five feet. If the entrance is decorated with shrubs and flowers, the board must also consider how those plants will affect the signage. Are they mature and not likely to grow significantly further? Will they need to be cut back to fit the new sign and if so, will they still look acceptable? If the plants are new, be sure they will never grow so high as to obstruct the new signs.

Many developments also have street and directional signage. **Local ordinances must always be reviewed prior to purchase to ensure any restrictions are met,** but generally signs on private roads *within* a planned development are not subject to the same constraints as those on public streets. Though the basic design and colors of stop and yield signs are well known, arrows no longer need to be black and white and street names often can be other than green metal with white lettering. Even though this freedom is a nice thing to have, it can be overwhelming and worse, it can create safety concerns. All directional signs, street name in particular, must be highly visible to police, fire and EMS, especially at night. Lettering should be done in reflective paint and should not be dark. Etched designs should have the highlighting necessary to make the lettering stand out. Some designs may be acceptable when additional lighting is added, although this comes at additional cost and maintenance, and may not even be available when most needed, such as during a severe storm.

Though entrance and directional signage may be replaced independently of each another, if the style of one will make the other look out of place then all should be replaced simultaneously to maintain a unified appearance. When doing so, take the opportunity to also consider if additional signs are needed (perhaps a yield sign or arrow) and also the location of the signs. If a plow routinely knocks a sign over or it is otherwise in the way of irrigation or blocked by shrubs and foliage, now is the time to move it, providing it will still serve its primary purpose in the new location. When considering adding signs, always remember that there is a tipping point after which anymore will make the property look busy or cluttered.

Rather than soliciting input from a homeowner committee, selecting new signs is one task which may be better for the board to work through on its own with assistance from the property manager. Though the board can certainly give parameters to a committee, aesthetics are a personal choice, and what the committee ends up choosing may not be to the board's liking. Unfortunately, as the amount of time and effort involved to select a design can be substantial, the board may feel cornered into approving a design they would otherwise not choose because they do not wish to offend the members of the committee nor restart the process. Further, the board is certain to be at least as large as any committee and thus it is as good, if not better, a representative sample of the views of the entire association. This is one case where the board should take it upon themselves to pick out the new style, keeping in mind that no design will be universally loved by the residents.

There are many firms in the sign business on the Internet with extensive portfolios that board members can peruse at their leisure, printing out those that catch their eye. With examples in hand, the entire board can sort through the possibilities, perhaps mixing and matching features until the group coalesces around a finalist. The property manager can then be directed to get sample sketches based on that idea from local firms. A small fee may be required, but often it can be applied against an eventual order. However, if a design which requires minimal change is chosen, consider using a reputable provider via the Internet – many of them are actually "local" business which are seeking to expand their clientele across state lines.

Perimeter Fencing

The discussion of the operation of pool facilities briefly touched on the subject of fencing. If the association is located in a fairly dense population area, such as a big city suburb, the property likely has some kind of perimeter fencing as well. Chain link was a very popular choice during construction booms in the 1980s and early 1990s and still is a choice today when builders look to cut costs. Chain link may also be used around storage facilities. Higher end associations are more likely to have some variant of aluminum fencing.

Chain link will eventually start to show rust and can lose its shape after run ins with trees and heavy equipment. A board faced with a large amount of chain link in decline has three alternatives. If the majority of the fencing is still in acceptable condition, the board can consider touching up the bad sections with an appropriately colored paint. This can be done by a handy man in short order with the use of a brush, roller or spray can. But this type of touch up will quickly become impractical as the affected area increases. For larger sections it will be more cost-effective to install new chain link while keeping the existing posting (straightening as necessary). A competent handy man and assistant should be able to do this kind of work but if the board is at all uncertain, retain a local fencing company. The work will be done correctly, though at a premium to the handyman and possibly with pressure to replace more fencing than is necessary.

If the board and property manager feel the current fencing is past the point of reclamation or simply desire to improve the look of the property, then the third alternative, complete replacement, applies. The board must understand up front that although replacement is not the most complicated capital project, the cost can be substantial and escalate very rapidly depending on the materials used.

The initial step is to have the property manager review the local ordinances which can place restrictions on materials and heights that were not in force when the association was constructed. The property manager should also contact a local fencing firm to provide a quick estimate on the cheapest alternative, chain link. This may not even require a visit to the property if the property manager can provide a good estimate of the number of feet of fencing required. With this figure in hand, the board will quickly know whether they are able to proceed at all and if so, whether more expensive alternatives can be considered. The board may find they must shelve the project for a number of years, reserving the necessary funding from common charges, special assessment or some combination. A small bank loan may also be an alternative if the short fall is expected to be made up in the next calendar year, but *it is not appropriate to saddle the association with long term debt to replace a functional but unattractive fence.*

Assuming funds are available, there are many, many choices available in aluminum and wrought iron. In most cases, aluminum is to be preferred over wrought iron. Aluminum fencing should require no maintenance (painting, rust treatment, etc.), and is available in multiple grades, from light residential to very sturdy industrial. If security is the paramount consideration, wrought iron should be considered. Wrought iron may also have additional styles and customizations available and will give a more historic look. Aluminum, however, is easier to install and because it comes in relatively small sections, can be far cheaper to repair or replace if damaged by downed trees or cars. Aluminum fencing is also easier to work with on a property which has hilly or sloping terrain.

Because it is very easy to be caught up in a cycle of "but that really looks a lot better ...," it is advisable for the board to set a target cost and a maximum cost which is acceptable early in the process. *Never lose sight of the primary functional role of the fencing and always ask "Is this good enough?"* The association has many on-going capital requirements which should not be short changed in an effort to pick the most beautiful fence rather than the nicest that fits the resources the board can allocate to the project.

Lighting

Site lighting is an important part of any property – both as a potential financial drain as well as its ability to enhance safety. Lighting comes in many varieties, from tall poles to spot lights to round disks attached to buildings and fence posts. In addition to styling, bulb and associated electronics are also varied, ranging from traditional incandescent to LED to induction.

Most older, pole based lighting are of the high pressure sodium or metal halide/mercury vapor type and have a ballast to jump start and power the bulb. They are functionally similar to long tube fluorescent bulbs seen in homes or workshops. The lamp heads may have a metal top and plastic sides or a metal wrap around with a glass or plastic lens on the bottom. A light sensor is often located on the top of the pole or as part of the head structure. As these types of lights age, maintenance costs can become a nagging issue and drain on the operating budget with labor rates in excess of $100 per hour for a service call common place (more if a helper or cherry picker style truck is needed).

Cranky ballasts are the most common problem, and if the lights are cycling on and off randomly, the ballast is bad. Photosensors detect the ambient light level and trigger the lamp to turn on at night or even during a very heavy thunderstorm. Thus, a light which no longer goes on may be symptomatic of a broken photosensor. Or a broken ballast. Depending how the lamp head is constructed, water may be getting inside the unit with the result being shorts from rotting wiring causing the light to go on and off. Or it could be the photosensor. Or the ballast. Or all three, or some equally exasperating combination. Lastly, if the association was built in boom times and known to have a history of construction shortcuts, do not take for granted that the lights are properly grounded, if at all. As can be imagined, aging lights are an electrician's best friend as they result in many service calls. The association can easily spend $3,000 a year or more trying to keep most lights working, most of the time.

Some developments will instead have lighting mounted on the side of buildings and other structures (perhaps small posts). These lights, often called "wallpacks," can use incandescent, LED or halogen bulbs and avoid many of the issues discussed above. However, bulb replacement may be more frequent and sharp changes in temperature can result in broken bulbs. Wiring may also be an issue over time for those lamps which are powered using in ground cabling. This kind of lighting is more common in smaller developments where light throw is not a significant issue or rural areas where perceived safety is less of a concern. Still other developments, in more temperate climates, will rely heavily on ground-effect and spot lighting. These too are relatively simple to repair and replace but can be subject to abuse from landscapers, pets and even errant homeowners.

In addition to maintenance issues, many lights do not age gracefully. In particular, plastic coverings will yellow and become more opaque over time with exposure to the elements and sun. Degradation can be accelerated if cracks develop or metal coverings become loose. Poles can be damaged over time too – plows and snow can dent and bend them so that they are no longer straight, landscaping equipment can make dings from rocks and homeowners may even hit them with car bumpers if the poles were poorly situated.

The decision to do a capital project to replace the lighting results from a culmination of aggravation from maintenance costs, poor performance and undesirable aesthetics. For this discussion, the assumption will be that the association will stay within the same family of lighting, i.e., if it has poles it will stay with that; if wall packs or other ground based lighting, it will stay with those. A look at some of the commonalities of all the lights which board members should be familiar follows.

The *temperature* of a light is not a measure of how hot it gets to the touch. Rather, the temperature is a way to describe the frequency of the emitted light and is more generally known as the "color" of the bulb. In order to spare a lengthy discussion of the physics of light and electromagnetic radiation, just be familiar with this axiom: the higher the temperature the bluer the light, the lower the temperature, the more red the light. Counter intuitively, "cool" is a term used to describe the bluer, higher temperature lights. "Warm" is used to describe the yellower, lower temperature lights. Rather than the familiar Fahrenheit or Celsius scales, lighting uses the Kelvin scale ($0\,°C/32\,°F$ is equivalent to $273\,°K$ and $100\,°C/212\,°F$ is $373\,°K$). Warm bulbs are usually classified as having temperatures below $4,000\,°K$ with cool over $5,000\,°K$. $4,000\,°K$ is often termed "cool" white and is fairly close to a neutral white. $5,000\,°K$ is universally referred to as "daylight," but carries a more noticeable blue cast. A regular household incandescent bulb is about $3,000\,°K$, give or take. Although somewhat a matter of personal taste, most individuals prefer the warmer color temps to the cooler ones, which can come across as a bit stark. However, too warm a bulb may look unnatural thus the board should focus on lighting with temps from $3,500\,°K$ to $5,500\,°K$.

Closely related to color temperature is the CRI, or color rendering index. This is a measure that was developed to indicate how closely a light will reproduce the colors of objects it illuminates as compared to some standard light, with a value of 100 as most "accurate." Unfortunately, CRI is an unreliable measurement as multiple reference lighting can be used, such as $5,000\,°K$, $6,500\,°K$ and a blackbody (similar to a household incandescent bulb). Therefore, board members should not use the CRI when making a selection among candidate bulbs. The entire subject of color and color rendition is extremely complex and one which can easily confuse novices resulting in poor choices and the elimination of good candidates.

A very important attribute of a light bulb is light output which is measured in **lumens**. A typical 100 watt incandescent bulb used in a home outputs roughly 1,500 lumens. With lighting designed to be used outdoors for parking lots and large areas, manufacturers will often list the lumens per watt or lm/w. Part of the reason for using this format is to highlight the efficiency of the bulb – a higher output for every watt of electric power used saves the association money. As an example, one company offers an 85 watt induction bulb with an output of 65 to 90 lm/w. Note that the output can vary due to the fixture style and the color temperature of the bulb, so always ask the expected output for the exact fixture and color temperature the board would be interested in ordering.

Also of importance are the **photometrics** of the light and fixture combination. Usually presented as a graph (polar luminosity graphs), these charts show how the light output is distributed, i.e., how much is directly below the lamp, on the sides, above, etc. Many localities require outdoor lighting to have a cutoff or reflector to prevent excess light from going skyward (contributing to light pollution) and instead better illuminate the ground below the fixture. Terms like candelas (light intensity in a specific direction) and footcandles (the light that makes it to the surface) are also commonly used.

Ultimately, the board (and more likely the property manger) will be most interested in the luminance, as measured in footcandles, which hits the ground at the midpoint between poles or wallpacks. The IES is a standards group that gives recommendations to developers and municipalities and at this time they suggest between 0.2 and 0.5 footcandles average horizontal illumination for sidewalks in residential areas. Remember, this is an average figure, and it is necessary to consider if the illuminance at the point furthest from any fixture is sufficient.

Though it is easy to err on the high side (say 1.0 footcandles, which is recommended for commercial areas) the board must remember that these same lights will shine on windows and into the homes, possibly into bedrooms. Cutoffs can be installed to reduce that problem but depending on the location of the pole, a cutoff may also greatly reduce illumination where it is needed.

The board should also be concerned with the longevity of the lighting and its reaction to temperature extremes. As noted earlier, there are many choices but one that is gaining increased attention in residential areas is induction lighting. Induction lighting is similar to fluorescent lighting in that a gas, such as mercury vapor, is excited by the addition of energy to produce light. In a fluorescent light, electrodes with tungsten filaments are at each end of the bulb and an external ballast controls the flow of current into the electrodes. Unfortunately, these electrodes and filaments are subject to breakage over time. In an induction lamp, a magnetic coil is wrapped around one end of the bulb and this magnetic field is used to excite the atoms inside the bulb to produce light.

The key attraction of these induction type lamps are that they have extremely long service lives. Typical lifespans for induction bulbs are 65,000 to 100,000 hours as compared to 10,000 for metal halide, 20,000 for mercury vapor and high pressure sodium and 50,000 for LEDs. This has led municipalities to replace existing lighting with induction lighting in bridges and tunnels where any repair or maintenance work would cause significant traffic headaches. Manufacturers are now beginning to target the residential market with more attractive and appropriately sized lights and fixtures. Induction lighting is also very energy efficient as the bulbs output 60–90 lumens/watt and the electronic ballast used to power the electromagnet are up to 98% efficient – much better than those used with more traditional lighting.

As noted earlier, outdoor temperature can play a role in the expected lifetime of all lamps. Some do not perform well in very cold climates and LED lights will have reduced lifetimes if operated in very warm climates. Finally some attention should be given to the rated output over the expected lifetime of the bulb. Mercury vapor and similar technologies can see output fall to 10 to 20% of the original rating as the bulb ages. LEDs and induction bulbs appear to have the longest duration of high output with LED lights rated for 50 to 60% and induction around 70% of the initial output at the end of life.

With regards to style, wallpacks and ground based spot and flood lights are all very similar in appearance. Fixtures for poles are broadly broken into four categories: shoe box, cobra, bulb and coachman. Cobra are not recommended for residential developments and are most often used for highway and roadway lighting. Shoe box designs are often seen in retail parking lots and are square or rectangular, may have multiple boxes on one pole and can be used on a residential property. Bulbous designs are often seen on sidewalks and boardwalks and are decorative but less efficient as they do not usually have a cut off or reflector to keep light from going skyward. The coachman style is also decorative and will usually have at least a partial cutoff on the top to reduce vertical output. Expect to see a wide variety of prices: It is a good idea for the board to first review photographs of the various styles in many price ranges and then request the property manager to find additional choices in a specific price range for any styles the board believes are acceptable.

When undertaking any type of lighting replacement project, the board should request that all wiring and grounding be checked, fix any problems and if necessary, upgrade to current municipal building code requirements. This should be written into both the proposal requests and final contract with a price for installing new grounds, new wiring and repair or replacement of concrete bases if poles are used. Note that new poles can often use existing bases if an adapter can be found to match the current bolt pattern. If wallpacks are used, the cost to repair or replace and repaint any damaged siding should also be included.

Lighting seems like it should be a simple project but as can be seen from the above discussion, there are many pitfalls and technicalities which the board needs to be aware of. At the minimum, all board members should review these basics and use the Internet or other resources when further explanation is needed. The idea is that the board members will be knowledge-able enough to understand the proposals the property manager brings before them and also not be snowed over by a manger who does not understand the requirements necessary to ensure a good outcome. Finally, the board should not hesitate to con-tact the lighting manufacturers to discuss with them the project and the specific fixtures and bulbs proposed for use on the prop-erty. Manufacturer representatives are trained professionals and are happy to make sure that the association installs the most appropriate lighting.

Walkways

Walkways may or may not be the responsibility of the associ-ation, in whole or part. If the homeowners' agreement does not require the association to maintain sidewalks other than on common ground, the homeowner will be responsible for the maintenance and repair of the walk. Property maps should always be consulted to verify ownership of all portions of a walkway as the deeded portion of a lot may not always extend to the curb.

Individual homeowner sidewalks are most often the respon-sibility of the homeowner to maintain and any risk related to trip hazards should be theirs alone. However, the board must be cognizant of property boundaries and should have available copies of the property maps which were filed with local author-ities at the time the association was built. The board will need these maps to determine responsibilities when property lines run through walkways (which is not unusual). The board, possibly in conjunction with a homeowner architectural committee, should also establish what materials are suitable for sidewalk replacement. This information can be part of or referenced by the residents manual, and the property manager can provide the specifics on request to any homeowner contemplating the repair or replacement of a walkway.

In the situation where the board shares some financial burden based on the property lines, a review must be done to determine if the walkway does indeed need to be replaced and the exact percentage belonging to the association. If the replacement is purely cosmetic and the walkway is still functional, the board should refuse any request to contribute funds against the expense and instead, advise the homeowner they may replace the entire walkway at their expense. If the sidewalk is indeed in disrepair, the board should offer to contribute the funds necessary to pay for the association's share of the sidewalk if it were to be replaced in kind. The property manager should get an estimate from a reputable mason which can then be provided to the homeowner to establish the boards contribution. The homeowner may also request an estimate from another qualified mason, and work with the property manager to reach a mutual agreement on reimbursement. In any event, any such work should require notification be made to the property manager before work begins so they can ensure that homeowners do not use prohibited materials.

The board should also be aware that trip hazards are possible at the junction of the curb (if present) and the sidewalk. If a homeowner complains or the property manager becomes aware of this type of hazard, the board should arrange for a suitable repair at the association's cost. Though it can be argued this may be a case of shared expense, the reality is the association is most at risk from a liability standpoint, and the small amount of money involved is not worth a debate of whether the curb rose or the sidewalk sank. Fix it and move on.

The board should direct the property manager to do at least an annual review of sidewalks in and around the perimeter of the property. If deficiencies are found it may sometimes be possible to request the local municipality pay for and perform the repair. Even though the odds are low, it does not hurt to have the property manager make the request and in the interim, get an estimate from a contractor to make the repair at the association's expense.

Storm Drains

Storm drains are present primarily on the streets and in parking areas. The property manager should check the drains twice a year (spring and late fall) to be sure there is not an excessive accumulation of sediment or other debris which may result in over flow or clogging of the drainage pipes. Leaves, grass clippings, small rocks, pieces of asphalt and sand are all culprits that over time may clog up a drain. The board should also make sure the drains are not accessible by vermin or small children and pets. Raccoons in particular find the storm drains an attractive underground roadway and hiding place. The simplest solution is to attach a wire grill but more permanent and attractive solutions are available at additional cost. During the fall the landscapers need to ensure that foliage does not accumulate against the grills and block the flow of water into the drains or street flooding may occur in heavy downpours.

Fire Hydrants

Fire hydrants need to be flushed periodically by the water company, public works or fire department to remove rust and other corrosion. They will also check that the water pressure is adequate. If this work has not been done on a regular basis, the board should direct the property manager to make the necessary inquiries to put the fire hydrants back on the maintenance list. This is not a job for a handyman, and it should only be done by

Figure 3 Fire Hydrant Pressure - Coloring

Class	Water Flow	Color
AA	≥ 1,500 GPM	Light Blue
A	1,000 – 1,499 GPM	Green
B	500 – 999 GPM	Orange
C	< 500 GPM	Red

a qualified individual pursuant to any state environmental and safety regulations.

Fire hydrants should only be painted in colors approved by the local fire department. ***Hydrants in the United States are often color coded based upon the water flow available from the hydrant.*** This enables fire fighters to use the proper hoses for the water pressure at the hydrant and to select the best hydrant when more than one is available. *Only* change the color of a fire hydrant if it is *not* an approved color and only after having the hydrant checked by the fire department. Figure 3 shows National Fire Protection Association (NFPA) standards for color-coding (according to flow) that are used by most communities. Note that some municipalities require the barrel of the hydrant be painted a specific color and only follow the NFPA color guidelines for the top (bonnet) of the hydrant.

Group Mailboxes

Older HOAs may feel the existing mailboxes have reached end of life after exposure to the elements for many years. Current postal regulations specify specific standards for group mailboxes, also known as CBUs (cluster box units). CBUs are available over the Internet from many manufacturers. In fact, the CBU is the internal compartment which contains the locked mail compartments into which the mail is placed by the postal agent. The CBU is then inserted into an external housing or supports.

There are many styles, colors and finishes to chose from, and there should be no problem finding one that suits the look of the development. There are, however, a few pitfalls which the board should avoid.

First, make sure the design is preapproved by the US postal service. If it is not, the property manager will need to meet with the local post master and request a waiver. This should be obtained before any order is placed.

Second, consider both the height of the tallest box as well as the lowest box. Clearly, residents should not need a step stool to see or reach into their mailbox. But the board should also be aware that the individual boxes can be too low and require elderly individuals to bend over in ways that are unsafe.

Third, though some styles will offer pedestals or decorative tops, be warned that the paint used on those surfaces may not fade identically to that on the primary unit, and even if guaranteed by the manufacturer, a replacement three or more years later will no longer match either.

At this writing, a plain CBU with 16 doors and one or two package compartments (for drop-off of small packages like books from Amazon.com) should cost about $1,500 delivered. Installation can be done by any competent handyman with an assistant. A new sunken cement base is required and may necessitate the current box be removed and placed out of the way on saw horses until the installation of the new unit is complete. If space is available, the new base can be put near the existing unit. If the board expects to situate the new CBU in a different location more than 6" to 12" from the curb, the property manager should preapprove the location with the local postmaster.

Once the new CBU is in place, the property manager will again need to contact the postmaster to alert them to install the postal service lock on the front door of the CBU. Once this is done, mail will be delivered in the new CBU. Though it is customary for the regular postal agent to transfer any mail remaining in the old CBU, the property manager should also confirm that this will be done and if not, to make arrangements with the homeowners to remove their old mail by a certain date so that the old CBU can be disposed.

During this installation period the property manager should make arrangements for the distribution of the new mailbox keys to the affected residents. Most CBUs come with two or three keys to each door, and all copies should be given to the residents to avoid any potential privacy concerns. The ideal distribution process is by hand with a signature confirming receipt. Failing that, a package with the keys can be placed inside each box of the old CBU with the assistance of the letter carrier though not all will be willing to co-operate to do so. Avoid mailing the keys if at all possible.

If the previous mailbox did not have a package compartment, a note should be placed on the side of the mailbox explaining its proper use: the letter carrier will place the package compartment key inside the mailbox of the addressee, and after the resident retrieves their package, they should place the package door key in the outgoing mail slot. This method is preferable to leaving the keys hanging from the package door as they are easily stolen, placing future deliveries at risk.

Drain and Sewage Lines

At some point the board will encounter problems with the various drainage and sewage lines on the property. Drainage lines begin where the leader from the gutter enters the ground. In a row house style development, these individual lines will connect with a second, usually larger, line running parallel to the homes that directs the run off into a catch basin from where it will continue to an on-site retention pond or connect with the municipal drainage system. If the association is made of free standing homes, the flow may be directed into a shared line, a storm drain on the street, a dry well or some combination.

Ideally these drainage lines will all be a good quality PVC pipe but that is not always the case, especially for older developments. Corrugated metals or plastic commonly used in the 1980s tend to suffer from corrosion and also compaction as the ground settles and roots from trees or shrubs expand. If these are used on the property, the board can expect they will all eventually fail, and at some point, it may be more cost-effective to replace the service for an entire section of homes than repairing each individually over time. As pipes and conduits outside of the homes are typically HOA responsibility, the board will also be responsible for repairing any damages to patios, walks and shrubs while fixing the drainage issue.

Patio cuts are especially problematic and costly. In the simplest case, an existing concrete slab will only be cut wide and long enough for the PVC going away from the leader. When covered and patched, the cut out section is unlikely to match the color and possibly the finish of the surrounding original slab. This is likely to bring at least a few complaints from the affected owners suggesting that the board has hurt the resale value of their home. It is also possible that the new section will look better than the remainder. Complete replacement of any slab that is cut will accentuate differences from other slabs, though this will eliminate a cut line.

Clearly, the problems increase if a homeowner has put in a poured concrete or other decorative surface that cannot be temporarily relocated (such as pavers or blue stone). If the board is lucky, the material will be one which may be more easily matched. Based on these realities, the board will need to two track the type of repair which is done. If the homeowner has upgraded from the original materials used when the home was constructed, the board is obligated to return the surface to the way it was prior to the repair. For instance, if the patio remains original material and is concrete or cement, the board should try to match it as closely as possible but not concede to any homeowner demands for replacement of the entire patio. If the homeowner has upgraded the material to something else, the board is obligated to return the patio to its pre-work state.

A similar issue can arise if shrubs need to be removed. Often it will be possible to quickly replant the shrub, though for larger or older plants this may not be possible. There is also a chance the replanted shrub will be damaged or die at a later date. The board should be prepared to replace, at HOA cost, any such plants with new ones of the same type and if possible, of the same size or maturity.

In both the patio and shrub cases above, the board should be proactive rather than reactive. The board or property manager should meet with the affected homeowners prior to the start of work to explain the process and answer their questions. This can also lead to better accommodations when changes need to be made, such as when there is no identical replacement for a mature shrub. The homeowner and board can then discuss and agree on a suitable alternative. Similarly, a homeowner may be willing to replace the entire patio at their own expense, but they would like the association to contribute to the cost in proportion to the size of the area the board plans to cut.

Sewage lines are also subject to problems over time. Backups that are created by homeowner negligence are of course their financial responsibility. Usually the initial response to a backup is to have the homeowner call a drain specialist to come to their home to clean out the line (if they have not already done so of their own accord). The board will be contacted if the situation is recurring or if the drain cleaner determines the back up is not the result of homeowner misuse. At this point, the property manager should take over and attempt to get a good description of the problem from the homeowner and if possible, directly from the contractor they hired. With that information in hand, the property manager can then contact the association's preferred drain contractor to get an assessment of the situation.

The board should also be prepared to pay to have the line looked at with a video camera. This will cost on the order of $500 but will allow the property manager and drain specialist to provide the board with a more definitive answer as to the nature of the problem and recommend appropriate solutions. If the event homeowner negligence is found, they should be back billed the cost of the camera work and informed they are also responsible for repair costs if the work cannot be satisfactorily done by their own contractor.

Short of an actual break in the pipe, settling of the ground over time can cause dips in the line which leads to the pooling of waste water and an upward egress to the main sewage pipe. This situation may still allow slow, low volume flows of waste water to pass while faster, higher volume flows (such as from a washing machine, dishwasher, shower or toilet) backup into the home. Washing machine detergent can also be a culprit as the petroleum based soap residue builds up and constricts the pipe.

If the property manager recommends the replacement of all or part of the sewage drain pipe, the board needs to establish if there are any other homeowners in the vicinity experiencing the same problem. If settling is believed to be the cause, it may not be isolated, and it will be worthwhile to address all affected drains at once instead of individually at different times, especially if pavement must be cut. The board must be aware that a homeowner can accuse the association of negligence if, in the future, the interior of their home is damaged as the result of a backup from a cause which is known today.

The property manager should seek at least two bids for the work and ensure that the proposals received are completely comparable before distributing them to the board. If one contractor includes the cost of gravel or fill and the other does not, then the property manager should establish whether it is included in the stated price, and if not, why was it not included (or necessary)? Any pipe that is replaced should meet all municipal codes, but the board should also be aware that replacement of the entire run of pipe can be treated differently than just a section. For example, the building code may require that any new or replacement pipe must be cast iron but that a repair may be in kind. If the existing line is PVC, replacement in kind with PVC is far cheaper than using cast iron. Furthermore, because it is difficult to create a good seal between different types of pipe, the proposal may call for replacing far more pipe than is necessary.

When comparing bids, the board must also consider their comfort level with the contractors involved. If the price difference is not excessive and pavement will need to be cut, it is safer to pay a small premium and use the contractor whose work the board is familiar and trusts. The last thing any board wants to do is revisit a job six months later which involves digging up the street.

Contractors

CONTRACTORS HAVE ALREADY BEEN RAISED in discussions on other topics earlier in this book. In this chapter issues related to the selection, monitoring the work and handling major failures of contractors are discussed in more detail.

Selection

Much of the work of selecting the various contractors to do work on the property will fall upon the property manager. To an extent, the amount of involvement by the board or its officers in this process will depend on the level of trust the board has in the property manager and management agency. However, as projects increase in cost or complexity, so to will board involvement in the selection and vetting of contractors. Regardless of how comfortable the board may feel with the input given by the property manager, the board has the ultimate responsibility for all work done on the association's property and thus has a vested interest in making sure the correct choices are made.

Reputation is always an easy qualifier to grasp upon when comparing contractors. Board members may hear a familiar name, or one that others have said good things about, but care must be taken not to place too much emphasis on this one piece of information. Reputations are built up over many years and can often mask a decline in the current quality of work. This could be due to any number of reasons: new employees, too rapid expansion of the business or an economic downturn. Reputation bias can also result in the board unconsciously excluding contractors whom they are not familiar, potentially by-passing a better candidate for the job.

When the board solicits multiple bids, price can serve to exclude or raise questions about the bidders. If five painters bid on a job, giving four bids within 10% of each other and one that is 25% below the next higher bid, the board must ask questions. Why is the low bid so cheap? Do they do inferior work? Use no primer? Hire illegal help? The converse applies to a very high cost bidder. What makes them think their service is so special? Have the others omitted some important facet of the job? Has the board overlooked something as well?

It is critical that the property manager make sure that all bids are for the same type and amount of work and that the materials used are identical or nearly so. If there are differences, the property manager should note what they are, estimate the cost differential and get an explanation from the bidder why their proposal is different from what was requested. Many times there will be a good explanation – the painter may believe additional sanding is necessary or that one type of paint is better suited than the choice requested. The bids received should be complete, or they cannot be compared. If one drain contractor lists the specific types of replacement pipe, gravel, sand, etc., which will be used on the job and another bidder simply says "replace broken line with PVC pipe and patch pavement," it will be difficult for the board to determine which is the better bid. The second contractor may fully intend to use the same materials as the first, but without full disclosure the board is left guessing or gambling. There can be no assurance that attention to details in the bidding process will result in superior work, but most would view this as a good indication the contractor will stay on top of things throughout the job.

The board should avoid selecting (or asking to bid in the first place) contractors whose size is not commensurate with the job they are bidding on. A paving contractor who regularly puts down miles and miles of blacktop and concrete for government jobs is a less than ideal choice for the association's two parking lots and quarter mile of mile of roads. The board should not hire a painter with five or six employees who paint one or two homes at a time to repaint a 150 unit complex, no matter how beautiful their work. They just do not have the scale to do the job in a reasonable amount of time.

Finally, the board should, in conjunction with the property manager, review references with the understanding that most references given are likely to be favorable. Even so, by asking the reference specific questions, the inquiry will sometimes move past happy talk to achieve a more balanced assessment. On larger jobs, it can be well worth the time and trouble for board members to visit some of the reference jobs in person.

For instance, when evaluating painting contractors, much can be learned by visiting reference properties and looking first hand at how the job was done. Speaking to residents (who are generally more than happy to comment) about the contractor and their impressions of the results can raise issues of tidiness or poor work habits. Problems arising after the job was complete may also be revealed. The hope is that these visits will confirm the board's prior good expectations and prove superfluous, but not infrequently a bidder will be downgraded or eliminated from contention.

Monitoring the Work

The board should not be shy in asking questions about materials, as well as checking the work of contractors. Although the property manager may take on much of the day-to-day monitoring of the job site, the board has a deeply vested interest in keeping abreast of the situation. Often, more can be learned in five minutes with the contractor or their employees than thirty with the association's property manager. When in doubt ask, but keep the conversation to the point and as short as possible. This is a way for the board to get a quick progress update or the answer to a specific question, not to take charge of oversight or give the impression that is their intent. Direction should come from one individual, the property manager, not multiple board members.

In some situations, it may be necessary to maintain an active board liaison to make a quick decision or provide access to certain facilities. These kinds of arrangement should me made prior to the start of work. As an example, when painters have been hired to repaint the buildings, if a board member is available on-site, it can speed the process when the foreman feels permission is required before taking some minor action or a choice must be made between two alternatives.

Materials are another area where the board should be involved, though the timing of decisions can vary greatly. Some contract prices may be dependent upon the type and style of materials chosen. In other cases, the specifics of the material to be used may be deferred until the start of work, at which time the property manager will pass the board's decision to the contractor. It may also be necessary for the board to give final approval to the material before the remainder of the job can be finished. An example of a material that could be decided in the contract phase is the type of stone used to build a retaining wall. Color and specific style decisions might then be made subsequent to the bidding process. In a painting project, the board may request the contractor paint small areas of a home with two or three colors in order to give the board members a better basis to make their choice.

Materials that must be ordered, such as tiles, pavers or stones, should also be checked by a board member to verify that what the board requested is what was actually ordered and delivered.

The property manager can, in theory, handle these cosmetic issues as part of the oversight process, but there is always the potential for misunderstanding, particularly with colors. The time commitment is not large, but the success of the entire project may well depend on such simple guidance from the board.

Major problems

Although most jobs have small problems that are easily resolved, sometimes a project will suffer a major failure. If the board discovers or suspects a major problem, they should immediately contact the property manager. Do not speak with the contractor or their employees unless great damage to the property is imminent. The property manager will speak to the contractor and halt all work until the job site can be investigated and the situation conveyed to the board. If an engineering firm is providing the primary oversight, the property manager will contact them prior to any additional conversation with the lead contractor. The principal reason why the board should not discuss the situation with the contractor is to protect the association's position in the event of any future litigation or settlement. This is one time the board should leave all communications to the association's property manager and attorney.

In fact, litigation is probably the least likely outcome when problems arise on a large project. At the very least, the damages have to be significantly in excess of the costs of any litigation, the probability of recovery high and the amount the association could reasonably expect to *recover* if everything breaks their way, significant as well. It is quite possible for the association to "win" the suit but not receive a significant damage award and not have any portion of attorney's fees reimbursed. This may happen if the aesthetics of the job in question are the prime subject of the legal action. The judge may agree with the association's complaints but rule that *functionally* the work has met its goals. Thus any judgement may be far smaller than the board's expectation of being awarded not just the cost of the work done to date, but also the cost to remove what has been done and start over again.

The above example also illustrates why the board must be extremely cautious, ignore emotions and consider the potential costs and risks of any actions they have under consideration. Continuing the above example, because litigation can take many months, if not multiple years to resolve, the board will need to decide whether to halt the project until any litigation is complete; finish the project in the current manner (even though it is incorrect); or just back out anything already done and start fresh.

The first option is generally not feasible as it will leave an open worksite for a very long time, perhaps very close to some of the homes. The third option can only be undertaken if the board accepts the risk that the association may lose the litigation or only win an award which does little to offset the cost of the do-over, let alone recoup money already paid out for the original work. If the association has already paid $50,000 to the contractor and expects the cost of removing what has been done to be $20,000, the association is potentially losing $70,000 plus legal fees. If the attorney feels there is a 70% chance of winning 75% of the claimed damages, the expectation value of the award is $36,750. If the association's legal costs are $20,000 and the judge allows it to recoup half of that amount, the net award will only be $26,750 – far less than the initial $70,000 outlay and coming only after a very long wait.

Therefore, most of the time the board will need to come to some type of accommodation, bitter as it might be, with the contractor to complete the work and then move on.

The Management Agent

No FACTOR OUTWEIGHS THE EFFECT of the competency of the management agent on the day-to-day operation and long term well being of an association. The degree of aggravation and frustration the officers and other board members feel is inversely proportional to the ability of the management agency to be proactive, handle small problems without oversight, guide the board's decision making process and be responsive to the homeowners.

Even though focus easily falls upon the property manager(s) assigned to the association, problems pinned on them may instead be ramifications of problems within the management agency itself. Care must always be taken in delineating the major source of problems; a board can be fairly successful with a good property manager and poor management agency.

Contract

The primary purpose of the management agency is to provide, directly or indirectly, the services necessary to operate the association in accordance with its bylaws and homeowners' agreement. The language of most management contracts are boiler plate, with some personalization to suit both the capabilities of the agency and the association contracting their services. *All board members should be familiar with the terms of the contract so as to avoid future confusion and confrontations with the property manager.* If the board adopts the use of binders, a copy of the contract should be kept in the binders for quick reference at board meetings. What follows below in this section are descriptions and explanations of the services included in most contracts, though specific terms may vary.

Collection of Common Charges

The management agency is responsible for collecting regular common charges and other assessments approved by the board and will act in the name of the HOA by way of any necessary legal process to collect past due amounts, the attorney and method of collection by mutual agreement of the board and management agency. In addition, the management agency will provide the board with an itemized list of all delinquent accounts.

> *The management agency acts as a book keeper for the association and maintains a drop box service (mail or direct ACH bank withdrawal) for the association. Each month, the board will be provided with at least one schedule that shows the payment and receipt of common charges from the unit owners. One such report which is essential to have if a lien or other legal action is to be taken against a delinquent homeowner is a "tenant ledger." This report will list every charge to the homeowner and every receipt, ordered by date and with a running balance (or credit) due from the time they purchased a home and became a member of the association. As some homeowners may own multiple properties within the association, the report is usually on a per home basis.*

Unit Owner Complaints and Requests

The management agent will receive, record and consider how best to handle complaints and requests from unit owners and/or their tenants. Complaints are to be thoroughly investigated and any which are deemed serious will be brought to the attention of the board along with recommendations for resolution as provided by the property manager.

> It is imperative there be one central repository of all homeowner complaints and requests, and it should be with the management agency. Typically, each home will have a file which transcends ownership so that a complete maintenance and problem history can be maintained. The file will include correspondence between the homeowner(s), property manager, the board, attorneys and even contractors. Written documents can then act as backup to protect all parties involved. The property manager should also investigate all aspects of a complaint privately and not assume the veracity of any oral or written communication with a homeowner; this is particularly important when the complaint is against another homeowner.

Operation and Repairs

The management agency is responsible for assuring that the common areas, grounds, roads and structures of the HOA are maintained up to the standards deemed acceptable by the board and the bylaws. The maintenance required includes, but is not limited to, carpentry, cleaning, painting, plumbing and other normal work as may be necessary subject to any constraints imposed by the board. The property manager shall have a discretionary spending limit of $750 unless further authorization is given by the board, excepting in the case of any emergency repairs necessary to protect the property or safety of persons on the property.

The management agency will also act as necessary to ensure that unit owners are in compliance with those maintenance and repairs for which they are responsible in accordance with the documents of the association.

> The property manager is responsible for initiating the maintenance and repair process and the board should allow a reasonable figure for authorized discretionary spending by the property manager. As an example, the property manager should be allowed to purchase "No Diving" signs for the pool area if they feel it is necessary without first asking the board to approve the expenditure. The property manager is also compelled to check the condition of the individual homes or units and to notify owners

in writing, as necessary, to make repairs (for instance, to replace a missing window shutter).

Administrative Record Keeping

The management agency shall keep a comprehensive and accurate set of office records, books and accounts is in accordance with generally accepted accounting principles. All records should be available for examination by those individuals authorized by the board or associations bylaws on reasonable notice. Office records should include, but not be limited to, a list of homeowners and residents, maintenance records, and complaints and requests from homeowners.

In their capacity as book keeper, the management agency shall provide to the board every month a list of receipts and disbursement to and from the associations bank and various reserve accounts.

> *The management agency will handle the collection and disbursement of the association's monies and as such, must keep accurate records which can be used by a CPA to conduct an audit or prepare tax and other legal documents.* **The board should diligently read each monthly report to ensure errors are not made and to look for irregularities which could be signs of theft or fraud.**

Separation of Monies

The management agency will establish and maintain an account in an FDIC insured bank as custodian for the HOA and with the authority to draw upon it for payment of any obligations incurred in the performance of the management contract, including the management agency's fee.

> *It is customary for the management agent to initiate payments on behalf of the association without the need for the treasurer to sign each check. This is accomplished by adding at least one officer of the management agency to the signature cards on the operational bank account. Note that the board does not have to allow signature access to reserve accounts and may keep that authorization to the treasurer and president, though this is uncommon.*

Disbursements

The management agent is authorized by the board to distribute funds from the association's bank and reserve accounts on a timely basis to pay for for risk, liability and other insurance premiums as well as all regular operating expenses of the association.

> Because accounts payable are not entirely predictable and unexpected expenditures do occur, it is usually necessary to grant access to the reserve accounts to enable the transfer of funds to pay expenses in excess of the operating account balance or repay any overdraft protection drawn down.

Servicing Contracts

The management agency will arrange contracts for utilities, pest control and other necessary services, including tools and equipment as are necessary to properly operate and maintain the HOA. In taking bids and soliciting contracts for work, the management agency, acting as your agent, will secure for the HOA any and all discounts or rebates that are available. Terms and specifications of each contract should be reviewed with the board and if appropriate, multiple bids obtained.

> The property manager will routinely deal with the association's existing service providers or suggest new ones when necessary. When authorizing work to be done, the property manager is to negotiate the best deal possible (perhaps by prescheduling multiple visits for tree work) and any rebates or discounts are to go to the association and not the management agency.

Extraordinary Expenses

When called upon to oversee extraordinary repairs and/or reconstruction of the premises or to perform services not customarily performed by a management agent additional fees will be paid after negotiation between the board and agency of the hourly or project rate and the scope of services to be provided to the association.

The management agency will only do so much for what they are paid each month. Large projects which will require a contractor on-site for weeks, not days, will require additional payment if the board desires the management agency to oversee the work. Although the board may feel some what cheated, this is fair to both parties. The additional time commitment may be significant and the management agency may not even be a good choice to oversee the project. Instead, an engineer or architect may be the best candidate.

Transfer Manager

The management agency shall ensure that outstanding arrears are paid in full prior to the transfer of a unit to a new owner. The agency will update the appropriate records to reflect the new ownership and will make sure that any specific requirements, such as proof of insurance, are met.

*Whenever a property is sold, the management agency should be notified by at least one of the lawyers representing the buyer and seller so that they can have certification that all outstanding balances have been paid prior to the closing date of the sale. Doing so amounts to extra phone calls and paper work for the management agency, which sometimes leads to a fall off in diligence. In particular, the board should be clear that the only acceptable payment methods are cash or certified check, and that the check must be deposited into the operating account **prior** to the closing date. This is to protect against a bounced personal check or a fraudulent certified check. **Do not** accept payment out of the closing as the ownership will have changed and the association may find themselves with a legal nightmare trying to collect*

Compliance with Law

The management agent will do whatever is necessary to ensure that the association is in compliance with all orders, requirements or statutes affecting the properties and structures of the association placed by any government authority having jurisdiction and provided that the association is not actively contesting such legal requirements. In the event the management agency receives any order, notice or subpoena the board will be notified within one days time.

The reality is more likely to be a bare minimum effort. Management agencies will be aware of when a project is likely to require a permit from the local municipality and will know about significant county or state wide regulation changes (say to pool drainage), but beyond that the board should not expect the management agency will make more than a cursory attempt to stay informed. It would be wise for at least one board member to look out for mentions in the local papers concerning regulatory or permitting changes. The association's attorney is another reliable source of this kind of information.

Corporate Reporting

The management agency will work in conjunction with an independent CPA selected by the board to generate and file all such forms, reports, returns and statements on behalf of the corporate entity that is the HOA, as required by federal, state and municipal laws as well as the association's bylaws.

Working in conjunction with the association's independent CPA or auditor generally amounts to sending the auditor copies of the monthly ledger statements and the various board and committee meeting minutes.

Budget

The management agent will prepare for the board an operating budget for the next fiscal year and deliver the first draft at least 60 but no more than 90 days prior to the current fiscal year end. The draft will be based upon expected receipts and disbursements based on the current conditions with respect to arrears and any known changes in the costs of services and planned capital projects. After review by and consultation with the board a final draft will be sent to the board at least 30 days prior to the fiscal year end to be formally approved.

Yes, most management agencies will prepare a draft budget for the trea-surer. Often, the task is left to the bookkeeping department as they generate the various monthly financial reports. The property manager may give a cursory review and even specify certain amounts be added or removed to reflect the expected start or completion of projects. However, the treasurer, along with the financial subcommittee of the board, if it exists, should do a thorough line by line review. This is particularly critical if the association has recently changed management agents as they may not realize the current year actual for a line item is an aberration and not a previous budgeting error.

Board and Annual Meetings

The management agency will direct the property manager to attend regular monthly board meetings as well as the annual meeting of homeowners, if requested to do so by the board. The responsibility of keeping minutes of the meeting(s) may be with the property manager (or their assistant) or by the secretary of the association. The promulgation of the necessary notices to have a legally binding annual meeting will fall upon the secretary of the association; the management agency will handle the distribution of the notices, proxies and any other forms.

Some management agencies will act as recorder for the association at each board meeting and also the annual homeowners meeting. This is a very nice feature to have in the contract but only if the notes taken are of good quality. If the chore falls upon the secretary, it may be advisable to purchase a small voice recorder to provide backup to handwritten notes. It is not an easy task to participate, focus on the discussion at hand and also accurately record the pertinent points and who said them. Check with the association's attorney prior to using a voice recorder to ensure any notification requirements are complied with in full.

Professional Standards

The management agent will at all times operate in a professional manner and maintain the HOA to the highest standards possible consistent with the association's means. If additional acts and deeds are necessary, reasonable and proper, the agent shall perform them in conjunction with the discharge of his duties as delineated elsewhere in the management contract.

This is catchall to say the management agent and its employees should not be rude or deceitful toward the homeowners and the association's contractors. It also allows the board to make requests of the property manager that may not be specifically defined within the contract but which do relate to the property and are not "unreasonable" to perform. An example would be asking the property manager to research alternatives to cement walkways.

Miscellaneous

An additional schedule may be included related to the costs of producing reports, bulk mailings, reproduction of documents, etc.

This is where the association will be nickeled and dimed by the management agency in an attempt to pass onto the association as many of the costs of doing business as possible. The board may wish to question why some particular item is not included and review the fee structure for reasonableness, but there is little which can be done until the contract is up for renewal.

Problems and Solutions

EVEN THE BEST MANAGEMENT AGENCIES will at times have difficulty satisfying the board and association; the worst will rarely, if ever, satisfy even the most minimal requirements set forth in their contract. The vast majority perform somewhere between the two extremes but unfortunately, many seem clustered in a narrow range around barely acceptable. Of course, perceptions of the quality of service will differ from the point of view of the management agency to that of the board to that of the homeowners and residents of the association. Different associations using the same management agency can even have wildly different opinions of their agent; the same applies to property managers.

Management agencies will usually attempt to shift blame for difficulties to the board and homeowners, and there may in fact be times when they have a valid point. Boards will complain of "asking for the same things, over and over" and never feel as if progress is made. Homeowners are very sensitive to long waits for callbacks and even more so when treated disrespectfully or mocked. Property managers tire of the same homeowners calling about the same problem they were told cannot be solved to the point they are ignored.

This section examines common problems which arise between the management agent, the board, or the homeowners and offers potential solutions to mitigate or eliminate the difficulties.

Problem: *Property manager does not return homeowner calls and e-mails in a timely manner.*

This is perhaps the single most common complaint of homeowners. Nothing is more aggravating then having a problem that requires attention (broken gutter, water leak in parking lot) and never having the problem acknowledged or only after many days have gone by. Each delayed or non-call back increases the likelihood that future complaints will go directly to a board member and bypass an unresponsive property manager. As homeowners speak amongst each other, the danger for the board is that a perception, true or not, can quickly turn into a new reality where contacting the property manager is now viewed as a waste of time, and the only way to get something done is to confront a board member.

Solution: *Homeowner contact reports*

The board first needs to establish whether the complaints they have heard from the homeowner(s) are due to isolated circumstances or indicative of a recurring problem. It could be that efforts were made to reach the homeowner but failed. Sometimes e-mail does not reach the intended destination because of incorrect addressing or misdelivery to a junk mail folder. Voice

messages can be accidentally deleted and in-house phone systems can and do fail to work properly. Sometimes a homeowner
calls so often or is so rude that the property manager purposely
delays returning their call.

If a pattern develops over the course of 6 to 12 weeks, the
issue should be raised at the next regular board meeting during
executive session. Do not accuse; instead alert the property
manager that the board is concerned about reports of slow response to homeowner complaints and cite the known examples.
The goal here is not to shame the property manager or to put
them on the hot seat in front of homeowners attending an open
session meeting. Rather, it is to establish a frank exchange of information so the board can determine what steps, if any, should
be taken next.

Assuming the board is unsatisfied with the explanation(s)
offered by the property manager, the next logical step is to
require a log be kept by the management agency that records
all phone calls, e-mails and letters from the homeowners to the
management agency and their employees (property managers,
account managers, administrative assistants). The log should
be provided to the board at least once a month and prior to the
regular monthly meeting. If the association is large or there
is a relatively constant stream of calls and e-mails, then the
report should be made available bi-weekly or even weekly. Note
that sending the report to the board members requires little
additional work on the part of the property manager or their
assistant beyond that required to send any e-mail *as the report
itself should be updated in real time for each contact, not once a
week or once a month.*

The log should contain the date the contact was made, the
homeowner, the complaint or request, the date of any call
back(s), the date the issue was considered closed by the property
manager and a brief explanation if further research is required.
The board should resist the temptation to ask for too much information; the log is a summary report, not an in-depth review

of each and every call into the management agency. In reviewing the log entries, the board can decide if any merit additional explanation from the property manager.

A side benefit of keeping a homeowner complaint log is that the board can more easily spot problem trends and take more action as needed. If most complaints are about parking, come from many different homeowners and are not directed at the infractions of only a few, the board can establish an agenda item for their next meeting to discuss the "parking problem."

Problem: *Timely resolution of homeowner problems and lack of follow-up.*

A homeowner complaint log will assist the board in making sure the management agency is acknowledging homeowner calls and e-mails. However, a log alone does not ensure that concerns are resolved in a timely manner or that homeowners have been informed of the resolution. Along with the desire to have their complaints noted by the property manager, homeowners also wish to be advised when the problem is closed or what action will be taken to reach that state.

For instance, if a parking spot number has faded to the point it is no longer visible, the homeowner would most likely wish to know when the number will be repainted so they do not park their car there that day.

Another example is a homeowner who has noticed that an irrigation line is leaking and creating a swampy area. Depending on the severity, the property manager may get the irrigation service there the next day or the next week. But without a call back or other follow-up, the homeowner is left guessing whether their message was received. This can result in multiple calls to the management agency and unnecessary irritation to the homeowner.

Solution: *More guidance from board to property manager.*

If the property manager is simply not giving sufficient follow-up information to the homeowners but is otherwise on top of the job, the board should instruct they would like some contact be made with homeowners regarding the planned resolution of their complaints. A phone call, voice mail or quick e-mail with the pertinent information is all that is necessary.

However, if the property manager is taking a very long time to resolve complaints the board will need to institute the home-owner complaint log (if not already in place) with an additional column showing the actions taken by the property manager after the complaint was received. The board should also define a reasonable time frame for the majority of problems to be resolved, with the understanding that some may be more complicated or involve extensive work and specific board approvals. The property manager should be directed to adhere to that time table as best possible and if a resolution is expected to take much longer, to inform both the homeowner and the board. The positive effects of good information flow between the homeowners, the property manager and the board cannot be overstated.

Problem: *Property manager is inconsiderate in tone or language.*

The property manager will be subjected to the best and worst of the association's residents. Without doubt, some of these homeowners will try the association's property manager's patience (and perhaps the entire management agency) to the point where they may respond with bad language, tone or generally be inconsiderate.

Letters from the property manager, which inform a home-owner of a rules infraction or other problem, may be abrasive in tone and are viewed as disrespectful or insulting by the majority of homeowners.

Solution: *Additional board guidance*

The board should be informed if the management agency is experiencing a difficult time with one (or more) of the association's homeowners. If a homeowner is often abusive or uses foul language when speaking to the employees of the management agency, the board needs to step in and send a letter directly from the board to that homeowner advising them to cease and desist such behavior. Additional steps can be taken, if necessary, to further restrict that homeowner's method of interaction with the management agency staff. The board may also consider restricting the privileges of such homeowners.

An identical procedure can be followed if a homeowner continues to call about a problem or issue which has been addressed to the board's satisfaction or is otherwise known to be unresolvable. The letter should be on board letterhead and explain that further inquiries will go unheeded and that if the owner persists in contacting the management agency, the board may be forced to restrict their access to the staff. The overall tone should be polite but firm and if appropriate, include a summary of previous steps taken to resolve the situation.

The proverb of catching more flies with honey than vinegar applies to all communications with homeowners sent by the property manager or other employees of the management agency. Initial communications, such as warning letters, should be polite and non-inflammatory. Did the owner put the garbage out on the wrong day? A warning can suggest "Perhaps you thought the pickup was on Tuesday but in fact, Monday and Friday are the regular days. Further information can be found in ...." The letter should always close with an offer to discuss the situation further if the homeowner believes an error has been made or they require further explanation.

If the homeowner instead persists in the undesired action, additional letters can be sent and fines levied. The tone of each letter should be increasingly firm, but never impolite. The opportunity for discussion should always be available and reference should be made to any prior actions and letters on the same topic.

It is important to remember that homeowners *sometimes make honest mistakes* and treating these, at least initially, as such will build good will between the management agency, the board and the homeowners.

Problem: *Problems identified in common areas are not fixed in a timely manner*

The property manager is responsible for bringing problems in the common areas to the attention of the board and arranging for the necessary repairs and maintenance. Some items may be minor enough to fix that the property manager is expected to make those arrangements even before notifying the board. Yet it is not uncommon for the board to go through multiple monthly meetings before the remedial work is completed. This is both frustrating for board members and in most cases unacceptable behavior by the property manager.

Solution: *Bi-weekly status report*

When seemingly simple tasks are not being completed in a reasonable time (or without explanation as to why not), the board is forced to increase monitoring of the property manager and management agency. As an example, a request to correct a misbooked expense should be completed prior to the next monthly close. Getting a locksmith to replace or repair a lock to a door at the clubhouse should not take more than a week.

The board should request the property manager keep a log of all the minor work that needs to be done, including items brought to their attention by the board or homeowners at the regular monthly meeting. The level of detail does not need to be high – the item, start and completion dates and a brief comment on the plan of action or update to the status of work should be sufficient. The report should be e-mailed or otherwise delivered to board members every other Friday and the property manager should *update the log as events occur, not on Friday afternoon.*

The board may get pushback from the property manager and perhaps accusations of micromanagement by their superiors, but the board must be firm in demanding this report. Clearly there has been some type of break down, either with the property manager or within the management agency, to drag these small items out over many weeks or months.

In reviewing the report, the board may discover additional patterns. Are the delayed items only those that require the property manager to meet on-site with a contractor, vendor or receive a delivery? This could be an indication that the property manager has been assigned too many properties and is unable to block out sufficient time to be at the property. Another possibility is that the agent has been assigned properties over too wide a geographic area and is unable to manage the travel and visit time.

Patterns like those are likely to require that the board discuss the situation and then direct the president to speak directly with the property manager's immediate supervisor. This could require moving up the chain of responsibility at the management agency until a resolution is achieved.

The combination of the work status log and the property manager's report at the monthly meeting may also indicate the agent is simply disorganized, or again, has been given more properties than they can reasonably handle on their own. The larger management agencies may also have administrative assistants assigned to individual or groups of property managers. Is the association's manager getting the most out of theirs? A frank and open discussion with the property manager during the executive session may be able to answer some of these questions and help the board to decide what further action it needs to take, if any.

The goal is for the board to complete work on a reasonable schedule and the status report can assist to that end. However, if efforts are unsuccessful, the report also serves as the grounds for a contract complaint to be lodged with the officers of the management agency. Many contracts will have a provision that the agency has a specified period of time to resolve to the satisfaction of the client any issues brought to its attention, and if unable, the client is no longer obligated to honor the full term of the management contract.

Problem: *Failure to find competent or qualified bidders*

It will only take one botched capital project before the board never again trusts the judgment of the property manager to select contractors. Allegations of kickbacks and other favors from contractors to property managers and management agencies are widespread, probably more so than justified. Complacency is probably an equal, if not larger influence, in poor choices of contractors.

Solution: *Use local contractors and scrap any preferred vendor list*

Management agencies have preferred vendor lists for many different types of work. Property managers consult these lists that then serve as the basis for whom to send bid packages. Unfortunately, once a vendor is on the list. it can take a lot to be removed. Often, management agencies feel compelled to bring the lowest cost bidders to the association, presuming the board's prime constraint is cost, even if the agent knows the work performed may be inferior. Property managers also develop relationships with these "approved" vendors and believe they can get away with far less oversight of a project than if another, less familiar contractor is hired.

Realizing this, the board should *always* question the competency of contractors suggested by the property manager and should not rely upon recommendations from allegedly satisfied customers. Instead, the board should always suggest at least one name to the property manager for additional consideration. The property manager and board should not interpret this to mean that contractor will ultimately be the winning bidder; rather it is an additional choice and one the board may be able to fall back on if their due diligence of other bidders is inconclusive. It also puts the management agency on notice that they should not assume the board will automatically accept their preferred choices.

If the quality of smaller jobs around the property have not met the board's standards, they should expect similar performance from agency approved contractors on larger projects. The board should not hesitate to tell the property manager they no longer have faith in vendors on the preferred list and that in the future, new names will be required.

When feasible, the board should try to visit contractor references to both evaluate the previous work and when possible, to ask residents for their opinions. Board members of other associations may be cautious about giving a true assessment of the work done. Residents, however, are not worried about any repercussions as their statements are only informed opinions. The board may be surprised to learn that the painting contractor that the property manager is recommending was not very tidy, leaving paint on windows or shrubs. Or paving done after drainage work may show signs of significant settling, calling into question the long term quality of the work.

Another way to steer the property manager away from reliance upon a preapproved list is for the board to mandate that local businesses always be considered. Assuming they past initial muster, at least one local contractor should be asked to bid on each project under consideration. Keeping the work local can result in better prices and service for the association as word will get around the area to other potential customers if the job is not done satisfactorily. If the association could become one of their bigger clients, word of mouth between the home-owners and their local friends can be a powerful incentive for a contractor to pay special attention to the job.

Unfortunately, the property manager may only be famil-iar with contractors located far from the property, unless the association is lucky enough to employ a management agency situated in the same or a nearby locality. This is not to say a firm located 15 or 20 miles away will do a poor job, but they are likely operating outside their regular area and travel issues may come into play. In this case, the board must be willing to assist the property manger in finding reputable local vendors and contractors.

Problem: *Property Manager is a "Yes" man*

Property manager's must often steer a fine line between their responsibility to the association as a whole and maintaining a good working relationship with the board. When very dynamic personalities exist on the board, the property manager may fall into the bad habit of agreeing with most statements made by board members rather than arguing for what they believe is the more correct viewpoint.

Solution: *Frank discussion with property manager, board self-examination*

The board cannot afford to have a property manager who agrees with them simply to avoid argument. This is not in the best interests of the association or the board. When this happens, there are only two options available to the board.

The first is for the board to take a hard look at how they are interacting with the property manager. Do board members make demonstrative statements that put the property manager in the hot seat if they disagree? Do board members value their own opinions too highly? Few, if any, board members will have prior exposure and expert knowledge in diverse fields like painting, landscaping, drainage, pool operation, etc. Long time board members may fall into the trap of believing "This is the way we have always done it." But times do change, and what may have been common or generally accepted 10 or 15 years ago is now outdated or worse, viewed as incorrect.

The officers of the board should also have an open discussion with the property manager to re-iterate that the board *does* value the property manager's opinions and wants to hear them, even if they may be in conflict with one or more board member's own opinions. One way to ensure the property manager has a say is for the board to allow the manager to state the problem and a recommended course of action *prior* to opening the discussion to the entire board. The responsibility to ensure this procedure is followed falls primarily upon the president. After that point, board members should ask questions of the property manager's proposal. When a board member suggests an alternate course, it should be asked relative to the proposal put forth by the property manager – why is one way better than the other? What are the potential up and downsides of each? If the property manager has a well thought out course of action, the board should feel comfortable taking it by the end of this discussion. If they are not in complete agreement, the board can ask for the proposal to be modified to take into account their concerns. Alternatively, they can request that further information be gathered or analysis made before making a final decision.

Problem: *Property Manager minimizes all problems*

Water is bubbling up through the ground behind unit #4, a parking spot has caved in and the paint job from two years ago is starting to peel. Yet the property manager says "Don't worry about it!"

Solution: *Speak with the account manager*

Worry about it. Sure, there are minor problems that the board really should not be concerned about. But when everything is a minor problem in the eyes of the property manager, there is reason to be concerned. Whether the property manager is too glib or perhaps the other extreme, where every little thing is potentially a dire circumstance, the board needs to get the property manager back on track and giving them honest assessments.

Although the president could sit down with the property manager and discuss the board's concerns, this is a case when jumping to their boss may be the better choice. The account executive has a better knowledge of the personality quirks of the association's property manager and will be aware (though perhaps not willing to share) if similar concerns have been raised at any other properties. After the account executive sit downs with the employee to discuss style and presentation, the board should expect to receive far more realistic assessments in the future.

Problem: *Property manager and agency play favorites*

Homeowners are likely to be upset when they have the impression that certain persons receive favors, additional attention, faster response or other undue benefit from the property manager or personnel at the management agency.

Solution: *Evaluate and speak with the property manager*

Favoritism, real or perceived, can create a very divisive environment within the association. After gathering comments and examples from homeowners, the board should discuss the matter directly with the property manager to hear their side of events. Sometimes those who complain about slow service have contributed directly to the hold up. They may also be a chronic complainer who is never satisfied.

But it is also true that some homeowners may have established significant long term, positive relations with the management agency, perhaps even while serving on the board. As a result, they may receive some degree of preferential treatment since they are an easy client to deal with and have built considerable goodwill with the management agency.

The board must ensure that each homeowner is treated fairly and that none receive more benefits than their peers. That one may get a call back slightly faster than another is human nature. But it should not be the case that work for one is done at the expense of another, or that contractors *paid by the association* are asked to go above and beyond when certain homeowners are involved.

The board should reiterate to the property manager that "extras" are not allowed for any homeowners, and the scheduling of work should be as close to first come, first served as is practical given the nature of the job and the necessary approval process. As long as the property manager is giving all homeowners call backs in the desired time frame, the board should let them decide the order which they speak to the homeowners. The board should also remind the property manager that all requests, verbal included, should appear on logs or status reports so that the board is better able to verify that all are treated equally.

Problem: *Property manager fails to supervise contractors*

The landscaper comes every week, yet the property is not looking its best. Shrubs haven't been pruned, and some areas of the lawn have weeds. The pool water has looked a touch green during the summer. Does the association just have terrible contractors or are they not being adequately supervised? Is the landscaper waiting for the property manager to tell them homeowners have been notified about the pruning schedule? Did the pool maintenance man ask for approval to buy additional chemicals to treat the water only to wait weeks for the approval?

Solution: *Board member contact with contractors*

When board members interact on a more than fleeting basis with contractors, it is always a delicate situation with the management agency. Management agencies do not like having their authority over the contractors questioned or interfered with, and they especially hate "micromanagement" by board members.

On the other hand, the ultimate responsibility for the property belongs with the board, not the management agency, and one man's micromanagement is another's oversight. The board may get a lot of pushback from the property manager, but it is very important that at least one member have a relationship with each of the association's primary contractors and those working on special projects, such as painting.

At least twice a year the board member should have a brief conversation with the contractor or their foreman to discuss the work they are doing. Conversations should be friendly and informal. The goals are to establish a rapport with the contractor, hear directly from them if there are any potential problems to be aware of and most important, to make it known that they may contact the board at any time if they are unable to reach the property manager or have some other concern they would like to discuss. Give a business card or similar with a contact phone number and e-mail address at the initial meeting and reinforce that the board is available at any time, but that routine issues should go through the property manager.

If the property manager is present during these brief encounters, do not embarrass them by trying to get the contractor to contradict something they have suggested, and do try to make clear that the property manager has been keeping the board informed of the work the contractor is doing on the property. Until such as time as the situation is intolerable, the contractor should believe the property manager has the full support of the board and is the person in charge.

Eventually, the contractor or one of their senior employees will be seen without the association's property manager present. Take advantage of this moment of privacy to enquire if they are getting adequate support and direction from the management agency. Does the property manager return calls promptly? Are bills paid in full on a timely basis? Make sure to emphasize the board is available when necessary and they would appreciate a call if there are any problems or concerns with the management agency. This can, and should, be done without indicating there is any problem with the property manager or the management agency; it is nothing more than a routine check-up.

New Agent Search

THE BOARD IS EXASPERATED and has reached the limit of patience with the current management agency. Efforts have been made to work with the property manager and other agency employees to improve the level of service, but to no avail. Multiple property managers have been assigned to the association with no noticeable improvement. Now what?

Unfortunately, many boards will suffer through years of poor or dismal service due to inertia. Board membership may be in flux, thus it can take a while for new members to realize just how bad conditions have become. Others simply dread the work involved in a new agent search, and they fear that the association will end up with no better, or even worse, service after making a change. The board may even actively discuss how dreadful their current management agent is and even speak of the need for change, yet they never formally act to start the process of finding a new one. Eventually a breaking point will be reached, perhaps after a project is badly bungled by the property manager or enough homeowners are hounding board members with ignored or unresolved complaints.

The first step is to officially decide to start a search, with a motion made, seconded and approved. This can take place by an e-mail vote, a special meeting of the board or at the end of the executive session during a regular board meeting after the property manager has been dismissed. Remember to record minutes of any special meetings of the board.

Next, the board needs to consider exactly what they wish to gain by changing agents. To that end, the top four problems with the current management agency should be agreed upon by the board. Those will be the primary criteria used in the ultimate selection of a new agent. The board must be confident that, at the minimum, those four issues will no longer be a problem in the future.

Board members should then put forth the names of any firms they are aware of with any positive or negative comments they have heard. Using this seed list, the board now needs to determine the overall selection process, as well as which members will be actively involved in screening potential agents. A hypothetical example is shown below:

- Candidate Criteria

  - Office within 15 miles of the property
  - 50% or more of business is HOA based
  - Number of units of median property managed is similar to The Pines
  - At least five property managers
  - At least two accountants

- Outreach to determine if taking new accounts

- Request information package

- Review information and eliminate any obvious bad fits

- Prepare a universal list of questions for all candidates

- Schedule interviews

- Narrow choices

- Schedule follow-up interviews to include prospective property manager

- Final Round Table Discussion

- Vote to Select New Management Agent

A large board may want to split off a smaller group to handle the initial screening process based upon the candidate criteria. Even though the above cuts are only meant as an example, they illustrate important parameters. A board member may have a friend who lives on the other side of the county, 30 or more miles away, who raves about their management agent. However, if that agent's closest office to the association's property is also more than 30 miles away, the fit will not be good as the travel time is just too great. Today, even 15 miles can be a time consuming trek through suburban traffic, and the longer it takes the property manager to get on location, the less frequently they will be seen.

It is also a good idea to focus the search on agents who consider HOA management to be a significant portion of their business. Agencies whose primarily focus is condominiums or apartment buildings generally do not translate well to the typical HOA environment. A condominium association operates under more rigorous constraints than an HOA and often has an on-site supervisor available to handle small issues in lieu of, or at the direction of, a property manager.

Give thought to the size of properties (both physically and in units) that a management agency handles. If the association is only 30 units on three acres, it would be foolish to consider an agency whose median client has 400 units on 50 acres. The association would be minor filler in their revenue stream, perhaps even viewed as a training ground for newly hired property managers. The flip side also applies – an agency who only handles smaller associations may be overwhelmed by the demands of a larger association, especially if they have mispriced the contract.

Most property managers are assigned four to seven properties, dependent upon individual size and corporate structure. A large management agency will have many property managers and supervisors above them (sometimes called account representatives). A small or new agency may only have two or three. The board needs to be aware that property managers move not only between agencies, but also in and out of the property management business. If an agency does not have sufficient depth to handle the temporary loss of staff (property manager or accountant), the association and other properties under management are likely to see increased errors, omissions and reduced service until new staff is employed and brought up to speed. A smaller HOA is is likely to weather this type of service interruption better than a very large association where the demands on the agency are higher and it is not realistic for a board member(s) to pick up any of the slack. This may mitigate the risks of considering a smaller or start-up management agency if the association itself is not very large.

After making the first cuts to find the minimally acceptable agencies, the board should determine whether to contact the entire list or only a subset. In reality, the available options are probably not so great in number that further reduction need be made at this time, and in fact, the board may be chagrined to hear that not all management agencies are taking on new accounts or interested in their property.

When reaching out to the potential candidates, the board member calling should explain that the association has only just begun the search process and is now at the information gathering stage. If the firm is willing to take on the property, an information packet should be requested that provides details of the firm's history and operations, types of clients, etc. Also ask them to include, if possible, samples of typical monthly reports and letters to homeowners. Close the conversation with the assurance that the board will contact them again as the search progresses.

At this point, the work of the search subcommittee is done. The entire board should now review the information packets received from the candidate agencies, as well as notes which the searchers have taken on location, properties managed, etc. Avoid rushing the process and allow sufficient time for the busiest board members to complete their review. Only then should the president schedule a group discussion to air initial impressions and remove any bad fits from contention. If the remaining list has more than four candidates, the board should consider ranking the list, holding in reserve those firms rated below the top four.

The board must also formulate a list of 10 to 20 questions they feel are appropriate for all candidates to answer. The wording should be as unambiguous as possible to minimize wiggle room in the answers. If members have technical questions which are important but difficult to answer on the spot (perhaps related to accounting or other systems), group them together and forwarded those items to the candidates prior to the in-person meetings. Request that the representative be prepared to present the agency's response to those questions verbally or in writing during the meeting. This will avoid an additional waiting period to complete the interview questionnaire and make the interview itself feel more complete.

Some common interview questions are:

- When is the monthly report prepared?

- Are arrears updated prior to the monthly board meeting?

- Who takes the minutes at meetings?

- Who covers when the property manager is on vacation or sick?

- We want to define our own general ledger accounts, can you handle that?

- What accounting system do you use? Is it cash or accrual based?

- What is the preferred method for homeowners to report problems?

- How do you track homeowner complaints?

- We like most of our contractors, is that a problem for you?

- How often will you visit the property?

- What will you do when you are on-site?

- Who checks the monthly report for errors?

- What guidance will you give the landscaper?

- We plan to replace *(item)*. What experience do you have with that?

- Will you help us make a long term capital plan?

- Can you deliver reports to us electronically?

- How long does it take to pay invoices from contractors?

- Your two longest terms of engagement?

- Describe the HOAs you handle now;

- Our board feels our role in oversight is critical. Is that a problem for you?

- What background do your property managers have? What are your hiring requirements?

And a few less common questions:

- Our community is older and has special needs. How will you handle them?

- Our residents are Internet savvy. Are you?

- Your firm is small. What succession plans are in place if the owner dies or is incapacitated?

The last question above is actually an important one and is likely to catch the firm's representative off guard. The board should not be shocked to hear "We've never been asked that before!" Their succession plans may be sketchy, at best. Most property management firms begin with an individual or partnership and gradually add staff as they take on more accounts. Too often little thought is given to the possibility that the owner or senior partner may be killed in a car crash or have a heart attack. Is the surviving partner authorized to assume the presidency? If there is no partner, which member of the staff will take charge? Will the heirs keep the firm in business (if they are financially able to do so)? Clearly, *someone* must take charge as leader of the firm if it is to remain viable. Thus, succession is not without repercussions for the accounts under management who may find they need to employ a new agency on very short notice. For the board, this may be the question and answer that breaks a tie between two equal candidates.

When it is time for the actual interview, the president of the board should lead the discussion, with the routine questions split between all the board members to allow each to interact with the representative of the management agency. Follow up questions should be encouraged but not to the point of bogging down the discussion on minutiae which may best be addressed in writing later or at a follow-up interview. The board should also give the candidate an idea of the remaining selection process and time-frame to come to a decision.

Board members must remember that they are listening to a sales pitch during the interview. Every agency will sound wonderful during their introductory remarks, and answers will be phrased to put the best light on their firm. Responses may also be keyed to the tone or wording of questions. The representative will tell the board what they think it wants to hear, while not straying too far from corporate reality to be tripped up later on. Board members should be polite, but direct and business-like in their questioning. Remember, this is not about making a new friend, extolling the virtues of the property or otherwise impressing the candidate agency. Instead, treat it as hiring a new employee in an office or selecting the vendor of some good or service. When a statement sounds too good to be true, do not let it go unchallenged but again, do so in a professional, polite manner. This should lead to less sugar coated answers as the interview proceeds. If it has not already done so, the management agency should provide the board with the proposed cost of their services during this meeting.

The board should again allow a week or two after the initial interviews are complete to gather their thoughts and opinions of each candidate and then schedule a meeting to exchange views. The time gap is essential to avoid having the last one or two interviews overwhelm the discussion because they are still freshest in mind. The president needs to make sure each agency gets a fair shake. The president may start the discussion by asking "What are the two things you like best and least about this firm?" This will bring some focus to the comments and avoid a rambling list from each member. The secretary should keep a list of the noted positives and negatives for each agency. Before continuing further, the president should review the summary for each agency and move whether each are due additional consideration or should be dropped now. This is *not* meant to be the final selection, but instead is a way to eliminate any agency which has made a poor impression, at least relative to its competitors.

The goal of the second part of the discussion is to determine what additional questions the board members have for each agency or the entire candidate pool (perhaps there is an area of concern which was missed earlier). As the final interview should be with a property manager, ideally the one the agency would assign to the association, board members may have very specific questions related to their education, time in the business, prior employment, etc.

One of the board members from the search committee should schedule the final interview for the remaining candidate agencies. They should request that the only representative attending be the property manager most likely to be assigned to the association's property. If there is significant pushback against this, allow the interview to go forward and decide later if this is indicative of a lack of trust in the judgement of their employees. The interviews should closely follow the format used in the initial meeting and again, time allowed for impressions to settle after the final one is complete before the board next meets.

The board will next convene for a final meeting when they will discuss the second interviews and ultimately chose the winning candidate. Once again, make a list of pluses and minuses for each property manager, and combine this with the earlier summary for each agency from the first interview. Ironically, cost is unlikely to be a major item in the final discussion if the association is in a urban or suburban setting where there is significant competition between management agencies. Instead, the focus will likely fall into three areas: a) which agency seems to be the best fit? b) which agency appears to be most professional, competently operated and brings the most to the table? c) gut feelings.

What is a good fit? It could be an agency that manages many properties with very similar characteristics to the association. It could be the impression that the agency views management of the property and associated problems the same way the board does. Will the property require major capital projects over the next five years? If so, an agency that has good experience managing that type of work could be the best fit even if it has short comings in other areas.

Each agency as its own style – some will give a clear impression they operate by the seat of their pants while others seem to have plans in hand and run like a well oiled machine. Some may appear to be stuck in yesteryear and barely in the information age while their competitors have incorporated new technologies into their business and will continue to do so in the future.

Gut feelings will also come into play. On paper the agency may appear a winner, but something deep down pushes board members to harbor unspecified doubts. This intuition should not be discounted in the decision process. Better to take the second choice with full confidence, than a first choice that leaves many board members with nagging doubts.

There is a great temptation for board members to place too much emphasis on the property manager they liked best in the final round of interviews. This could be based on responses to the questions, their skill set, or even their personality and "fit" to the style of the board. But the board is not hiring just the property manager, they are hiring an entire team. An exceptional interview should not eliminate concerns about the agency as a whole. Property managers turn over frequently and may also be reassigned: *a board who selects only on the basis of the property manager may have deep regrets in the not so distant future.*

Once all thoughts and feelings have been aired, the president should call for a secret vote to select the preferred candidate. If there are more than two competitors, the president may ask to take multiple votes until only two candidates remain, so ensuring the winner has a majority vote among the board members. A secret ballot is necessary to allow each member to cast their vote without peer or other pressures, real or perceived.

No notifications should be made to the losing candidates

until a contract is signed. The runner-up should be considered as the fall back were there to be a failure to agree on terms with the desired agency. Although this may sound unlikely, it allows the board to continue to negotiate from a position of strength and if necessary, does not make future negotiations with the runner-up awkward.

The president must now notify the winning candidate and begin contract negotiations. These negotiations may include the annual cost, inclusion of requirements, such as status reports or contact logs, or any other items the board feels are missing from the agency proposal. The association's attorney will play a major role and handle the majority of the contract review and negotiations, often attempting to put more stringent requirements and language into the contract to protect the association. When the final version is agreed upon by both sides, the president should circulate a copy to the remaining board members for review. Members must then meet either in person to grant approval or by e-mail with follow up confirmation at the next regular meeting. Once signed, all other bidders should be notified of the results and thanked for their time and effort.

Termination

BEFORE FORMALLY AWARDING THE MANAGEMENT CONTRACT to a new agency and giving notification to the current agent, the board first needs to discuss and agree upon a number of items: the date of the termination notice, the date the transition must be complete, how homeowners will be notified, and the effect, if any, on outstanding projects. In fact, some of these items may even have influenced the timing of the search for a new agent.

A review of the existing contract will show the minimum notice that must be given to the current agent; 60 and 90 days are common. Though not essential to do so, consideration should be given to timing the notice and end dates to coincide with either a quarter, semi or fiscal year end (most HOAs use a calendar year end for the fiscal year). The ideal changeover usually will be calendar year. This will give a clean set of books to the new management agent beginning January 1. This time of year is also generally a quiet time for many associations, in particular those in the snow belts. If the association is located in Florida, Arizona or another location that may see an influx of second homeowners for the winter months, additional consideration for a December 31 changeover may be required if it would interfere with the smooth operation of the property.

Keep in mind that a management agency which has shown itself to be disorganized and unmotivated is unlikely to put much effort into a transition that can involve getting file boxes out of storage, transfer of paper and digital records, and the transfer of the general ledger structure and history of a soon to be *former client*. If the association can absorb the relatively minor cost and the new management agency is able to do so, try to arrange for a one month overlap between the take over by the new and termination of the old agents. This will make it easier for the new management agency to wrap up any loose ends with the current firm. It also allows homeowners and vendors a one month buffer before all payments and invoices must be sent to a new address or risk rejection.

Major projects can complicate the question of when to terminate. If a major project has not yet begun, can it be delayed by 60 or 90 days to allow the new management agency to take charge? If the project is already underway, will it be completed prior to changeover? Much of the thought process here is to decide if the oversight by the management agency is essential to the successful completion of the project, or if it is sufficient to allow one (or more) of the board members to assume that role. The board may determine that circumstances require they retain the current management agency until the project is complete and the association should *not* serve notice on the current management agency until that time.

A poor alternative would be to engage the new agency on a consultancy basis to pick up oversight in the middle of the project – any stumble on their part may affect the changeover and permanently sour the future relationship. However, a project that can be delayed, or has been planned to start co-incident with the changeover, is acceptable as the new agency will have ample time to review the project, contractors, etc., and request any changes they feel are necessary.

Once the board has established an acceptable termination date, the president must contact the association's attorney to discuss the impending event. The attorney will do a review of the existing contract to make sure any and all preliminary notifications have been met and will likely have some recommendations of their own on the transfer of responsibilities. The president should request that the attorney prepare two letters on behalf of the association.

First, the initial termination notification which will be sent to the current management agency by fax and overnight mail on the appropriate date. A second letter to the current agent, notifying them that the new management agent has assumed day-to-day responsibility of the association, should be prepared and delivered at a later date. This letter should also state that there are to be no further transactions in the association's bank or other asset accounts and that any documents not yet turned over to the new management agency should be transferred immediately.

Finally, the board needs to prepare a notification to the homeowners, including those who rent their units. The letter should be brief, no longer than a page. In it, the board should touch briefly on the reasons for leaving the current management agent. The bulk of the letter should focus on the new agent and the board's optimism for better management of the property. Also include an outline of the time table for the transition and indicate that until otherwise notified, all payments and complaints should still be directed to the old management agency. Close the letter with word that the new management agent will contact them with additional information, including a date for a meet and greet with the new property manager.

This is one letter the board will need to deliver on their own. With the expectation that the current management agent will receive their termination notice at the start of the business day, the board should arrange to hand deliver the homeowner notice during the morning hours. Board members should be prepared for questions but may be surprised not to receive very many. A switch is probably not a shock to the residents, many of whom are aware of or have been on the short end of sub-par performance from the current management agency. Their questions are more likely to be forward looking and are best met with a "stay tuned" response. All residents will receive several communications from the new agency before the official changeover date that will answer most, if not all, of their questions.

Going forward, the board must check in periodically with the new property manager to assess how smoothly the transition is going and if any assistance from the officers of the board is required. Access to the association's attorney should also be granted (with written notification to the attorney) so that legal and other questions can be addressed in a timely manner. This is also the time for the board to lock up the day of the month for the regularly scheduled board meeting with the new property manager.

One of the more annoying transition tasks is completing the documentation related to the operating and reserve bank accounts. Regardless of whether any of the accounts are kept open, new signature cards will be required to allow access by the new management agency. If the board is happy with its current banking relationships, they should ask the new agent to keep the accounts open but for security, change the account numbers. If the board only has one or two accounts and no particular attachment to the financial institutions, authorization can be given to the new management agent to open the appropriate accounts with their preferred banking institution, provided the credit rating is good.

After the transition is complete, the treasurer must closely review the first monthly report generated by the new agent. Opening balances should be identical to the closing balances of the prior report. Even though general ledger account numbers may be different, the account titles should be similar, and if any additional accounts were requested, they should be included in the new financial statements and have the correct budgeted amounts. The treasurer also needs to review the journal entries for the current month to be sure the new agency is booking the transactions correctly. If timing allows, these reviews should be completed prior to the first regular monthly meeting so that the remaining board members can receive corrected financial statements.

During the initial three to six months after the transition, the board can expect to provide more guidance than normal to the new property manager. The property manager will be feeling out not just the homeowners but also the board's priorities, internal dynamics and preferences for handling run of the mill problems. The board should certainly expect new ideas and view points to be presented by the property manager and must allow them the freedom to pursue their preferred methods unless the board has a demonstrably good reason to take a different course of action.

An example of when the board might ask the manager to defer to their judgement is on how to handle certain homeowners. The board may have the knowledge of past events and issues which color the relationship in a way that the property manager would be unable to determine on their own. This knowledge can prevent the new property manager from inflaming a delicate situation unknowingly.

There is a fine line between getting up to speed and failure to do the job properly, thus the board should not hesitate to speak with a senior manager at the new agency if they sense potential problems developing. If such a discussion takes place, make it one which encompasses the entire transition, taking time to give positive reinforcement where the board has seen strengths or been impressed by the suggestions and actions of the property manager. When the conversation turns to the real reason(s) for the meeting, avoid passing judgment, and instead, first ask why things were handled the way they were. If the explanation is not convincing or some doubts remain, take this opportunity to explain why the board has concerns. The objective is for both parties to work to to right the course of the relationship early on to prevent future disappointment, animosity or misunderstandings.

Budgeting

Where Has All The Money Gone?

THE RESPONSIBILITY FOR PREPARING the association's budget falls upon the property manager, the treasurer, the president and any other board members who are on the finance committee, if one exists. Once approved, the budget will be entered into the management agency's general ledger system and used in the monthly financial reports distributed to the entire board (see *Appendix B* for a sample report).

Operating Budget

Preparation of an operating budget outline, based upon the prior and current year general ledger balances, is a fairly straight forward exercise for the property manager and accounting clerks within the management agency. This initial framework will be delivered to the treasurer and president after which they may bring in other members of the finance committee.

The first order of business is a review of the prior and current years to date. The budget principals should note any items that may have been exceptional or one time expenses, such as the unexpected replacement of an air conditioner in the clubhouse or extra tree service after a very severe storm. The objective is for the budget to reflect the baseline, normal operating expenses of the association. Elevated or reduced funding due to anticipated changes should also be reflected in the operating budget. Such changes could reflect periodic services, such as every other year tree pruning, a new landscaping contract, a special assessment or just general adjustments for inflation. If board members or the management agency are new, it may be necessary to ask long term or even past board members to comment on prior year expenses so as to identify any unusual expenditures and circumstances.

The general ledger itself needs to show sufficient granularity so expenses are accurately portrayed. Having one line item for "pool" will not be of any help in explaining a $7,000 overage nine months later. Break the accounts down to a level that is informative but not excessive. For a pool, a split into chemicals, pool supplies and management contract is probably sufficient. There should be no need to break down the chemicals and routine pool supplies further into additional line items. For landscaping, there should be an item for the base landscape contract and additional line items, as necessary, to reflect annual flower expenses, expected shrub replacements, storm cleanups, etc. If the property manager or their accounting staff complain, stand firm as these are the association's books, and the board is entitled to have financial information presented in any manner it feels is accurate and helpful to operating the association. It is possible that some accounts should be removed; remember that it will take two years for those to fall off reports because of the need to show the current against the prior period.

The treasurer should strive to ensure there is an operating reserve account funded with 2% to 3% of the total income of the association. In addition, a storm reserve account should be funded with 10% of the base landscape contract or $15,000, which ever is larger. The operating reserve handles unexpected items that may pop up over the course of the next year, such as the replacement of an air conditioning system in a clubhouse. The storm account is one the board hopes never to use but will be thankful to have in the event of severe tree or property damage after a storm. Remember, the rates charged by landscapers and arborists for emergency cleanups can be considerably higher than regular or off-season rates. A severe storm can easily result in $30,0000 to $50,000 in cleanup costs, even if much of the cleanup is left until rates are normal again. Often overages in some accounts will be offset by similar favorable underruns in other accounts. At the end of the year, all excesses and shortfalls will net through the regular reserve accounts.

Capital expenses can be reflected in the general ledger in a number of different ways. One common way is to include these items at the end of the operating budget statement. The treasurer should provide the property manager, in writing, the details of any capital projects approved by the board for the next year and based upon the capital budget (see below). If any assessments or loans will be necessary, those too should be reflected in the operating budget. Many ledger systems will report a "net income" for the association as an excess of sources of funds (common charges, assessments) over all of the expenses. This is, in fact, the balance that is available to either fund capital projects or be held in reserve. Sometimes it may be necessary to work backward from this figure, for instance when reserves have been depleted and must be built up again, the treasurer may demand a certain dollar amount be withheld for the long term reserve accounts.

Capital Budget

A CAPITAL BUDGET IS CRUCIAL TO THE LONG TERM HEALTH of the association. Without some plan in place, the board is operating in fire prevention mode, always trying to fix the latest disaster with no idea of the cost of the next one. Assessments to make up short falls can be frequent and at times, shocking, to the homeowners. Without a capital budget anchored in reality, the board will always be flying by the seat of their pants and no operating budget will be worth the paper it is printed on.

There are two stages in the capital budgeting process: a fair assessment of the condition of the association's property, plant and equipment and then assembling that information into a format usable for financial purposes.

Capital Planning Report

Many associations try to wing it when it comes to estimating the remaining useful life of a roof, retaining wall, pool or the many other capital structures on the average HOA property. They inevitably also guess at the replacement cost, perhaps leaning on their property manager to make a "good" guess. Unfortunately, board members and property managers are rarely engineers or skilled contractors and generally are not in a position to accurately evaluate the current condition and rate of decay of these many items, nor are they in a good position to estimate future repair or replacement costs.

For these reasons, the board should engage an engineering firm which specializes in capital evaluations to produce a capital planning report. This report is used in preparing a capital budget for the ensuing five to ten years, perhaps longer. Like any other contracted work, the job should be bid out to three or four firms identified by the management agency. Most of these firms do other engineering work, so do not be surprised if the property manager is quick to bring a short list of candidates which have worked with their agency in the past.

The board should be clear of the type of product they desire as these engineers can do everything from a very simple report to an extensive document, complete with computerized engineering plans and specifications. The price will be dependent upon the size of the property and common areas, but an outlay of $10,000 to $20,000 should give most associations a pretty extensive look at the property and a detailed write-up of its current condition, problem areas and estimated current replacement costs.

During the interview process, the board and property manager should explain what type of report and analysis they require. Once the engineer is chosen, the president and property manager will sit down again with the engineer to convey any areas that they feel deserve greater attention prior to the start of their work. At this price level, most of the evaluation is done by eye and hand. If the board has special concerns regarding pipes and drains, be prepared to pay additional charges for samples and other underground evaluation techniques. All such plans and fees should be discussed and agreed upon in principle *prior to signing the official contract.*

A typical inspection will look at the roadways, parking lots, curbing, sidewalks, retaining and perimeter walls, fences, gates, lighting, storm water drainage, roofing, clubhouse and associated amenities (pool, tennis courts, etc.), and various miscellaneous items. The finished report will usually include photos, descriptive text, detailed evaluation of the current conditions and if problems exist, the probable source, an overall grade (i.e. good, fair, poor, unsafe), and an estimate of the cost to replace or repair the item. When appropriate, each grouping will be further broken down. For example, the condition of roadways may vary greatly and thus be subject to differing remaining life as well as differing costs to repair. For an HOA on 10 to 25 acres with 100 to 200 units, the report will be the order of 50 to 100 pages.

The engineer will often prepare a preliminary report that is sent to the property manager, president and any other board member or resident who has been involved in the project. If items are missing or the presentation is not clear enough, this is the time to fix it. It is also a good idea to ask the engineer to prioritize the required work within each area. Once blessed by the review group, the final report is generated, copies delivered to the board (perhaps both in print and electronically) and

232 A FRAMEWORK FOR HOA MANAGEMENT

a summary meeting with the engineer is scheduled. At that meeting, board members should ask any questions they may have about the findings in the report, paying close attention to priority items in the context of the association's ability to pay for remedial work in the near to medium term. The engineer can help guide the board in how best to allocate the association's limited funding.

This report truly belongs to the association, not just the board, so it should be distributed to the entire membership. This will serve both to inform the homeowners of the real condition of the property and also make it far easier for the board to move forward with a long term plan to handle the repairs and maintenance described in the report. Homeowners will have far less ground to question the wisdom and judgement of the board, and the necessity of the work it undertakes, as they now have in hand an independent assessment of the required maintenance and its expected costs.

Preparing A Capital Budget

With the data from the engineer's report (or some other reliable source), the treasurer, property manager, and finance committee, in whole or part, will meet to develop the first draft of the capital budget. This group will take the priorities and costs from the capital planning report and combine those with reasonable assumptions of how much of each project will be paid out of reserves, how much from a one time special assessment and how much via some combination of bank loan and assessment.

There will always be friction between those members of the association who wish to maintain the current monthly common charge, thus reserving little and adopting a "pay as you go" assessment approach, and others who feel most projects should be paid for out of reserves, even if it means a higher common charge. Those who only plan to be homeowners for a few years usually prefer the "from reserves approach" as they are able to reduce their obligation by the contributions of past and future owners. Those who intend to stay many years may prefer a one time charge that forces all current owners to pay in full now. This lessens the need for future reserve contributions and, in effect, lowers the monthly common charge.

In reality, 100% from reserves or 100% from assessment is impractical. Some projects, such as site wide painting, paving or roof replacement are so costly that any one time charge would be very large and quite possibly beyond the means of many homeowners to pay, even if given a year's notice. On the other hand, reserving the whole amount may result in a protracted period of very high monthly common charges and the delay of a project. Ignoring the ramifications of a long delay, larger reserves (and thus a higher common charge) can negatively affect the desirability of living in the community and make future home sales more challenging.

In practice, when preparing the capital budget, some common sense balance must be struck to decide how much of the cost of each project will come from reserves and how much from assessments. A $10,000 fence is likely to come completely from reserves as the cost is small and amounts to a *reduction* in the current year contribution to the reserve funds. A $100,000 project to extend the current irrigation system to include the front lawns of each home could be paid for completely by a one time assessment spread out over the course of a calendar or fiscal year. A $500,000 painting project will be paid for primarily from reserves, with any shortfall covered by either a one time assessment, a bank loan or some combination. Generally, the terms of a bank loan will require an assessment be in place to cover the required principal and interest payments. This extends a potential one time assessment over the course of two or more years, but it can ease the financial burden upon the homeowners.

Using a spreadsheet, a time line should be created going out for ten to twenty years with each year in one column. Each row will reflect one of the anticipated projects, with the estimated cost placed in the cell below the year(s) the work will take place. If the costs reflect current prices, they may be adjusted to reflect an anticipated amount of inflation using a reasonable estimate. A \$100,000 current cost could be estimated at \$128,000 ten years forward using an estimated annual inflation rate of 2.5% (\$100,000 x 1.025^{10}). Once all projects are entered into the spreadsheet, a summation is made for each column. The result is the anticipated capital needs of the association, by year, for the next 10 to 20 years. Figure 4 shows a basic capital budget spreadsheet.

The process is continued in similar fashion with the inclusion of ratios for the amount of the capital cost to be paid for out of reserves. New totals are generated that indicate the amount of reserves the association must have on hand each year to contribute to the cost of the capital projects. The difference between the actual anticipated cost and the reserved amount is the shortfall that must be made up by a special assessment, bank loan or some combination.

Using the association's current reserve balance as a starting point and including an estimated annual reserve contribution, the spreadsheet can be further extended to reflect the flow of capital funds. The result indicates years in which the association will have an excess in reserves and those in which it will have a shortfall. Ultimately, all shortfalls must be eliminated and in fact, a certain minimum level of reserves maintained. Besides being good fiscal policy, this is due to recent requirements the government sponsored mortgage lenders place on borrowers prior to granting them a loan to purchase a home in an HOA. The current figure is 10% of the association's operating budget. Modify the spreadsheet to include additional funds from assessments and bank loans (not forgetting to include the outflow when the loan principal is paid off). What is left is a reasonably accurate portrayal of the capital needs of the association and how its capital projects will be funded. Figure 5 shows these

Figure 4 Basic Capital Budget Spread Sheet

ESTIMATED COSTS

ITEM	2012	2013	2014	2015	2016	2017	2018	2019	2020	2021	2022	2023	2024	2025
FENCES	50,000	25,000	-	-	-	-	-	-	-	-	-	-	-	-
LIGHTING	-	65,000	-	-	-	-	-	-	-	-	-	-	-	-
RETAINING WALLS	-	-	115,000	-	-	-	-	-	-	-	-	-	-	-
ROADS	-	-	-	200,000	300,000	-	-	-	-	-	-	-	-	-
CURBS/SIDEWALKS	-	-	-	75,000	125,000	-	-	-	-	-	-	-	-	-
CLUBHOUSE/POOL/TENNIS	-	15,000	-	-	-	-	-	-	-	-	-	-	-	-
ROOF	-	-	-	-	-	-	-	-	-	500,000	500,000	-	750,000	750,000
PAINTING	35,000	350,000	350,000	-	-	-	-	-	-	-	-	-	-	-
IRRIGATION	-	-	-	-	-	-	-	-	-	-	-	-	-	-
TOTAL	85,000	455,000	465,000	275,000	425,000	-	-	-	-	500,000	500,000	-	750,000	750,000

RESERVES PERCENTAGES

ITEM	2012	2013	2014	2015	2016	2017	2018	2019	2020	2021	2022	2023	2024	2025
FENCES	100%	100%	100%	100%	100%	100%	100%	100%	100%	100%	100%	100%	100%	100%
LIGHTING	80%	80%	80%	80%	80%	80%	80%	80%	80%	80%	80%	80%	80%	80%
RETAINING WALLS	75%	75%	75%	75%	75%	75%	75%	75%	75%	75%	75%	75%	75%	75%
ROADS	70%	70%	70%	70%	70%	70%	70%	70%	70%	70%	70%	70%	70%	70%
CURBS/SIDEWALKS	70%	70%	70%	70%	70%	70%	70%	70%	70%	70%	70%	70%	70%	70%
CLUBHOUSE/POOL/TENNIS	100%	100%	100%	100%	100%	100%	100%	100%	100%	100%	100%	100%	100%	100%
ROOF	70%	70%	70%	70%	70%	70%	70%	70%	70%	70%	70%	70%	70%	70%
PAINTING	70%	70%	70%	70%	70%	70%	70%	70%	70%	70%	70%	70%	70%	70%
IRRIGATION	100%	100%	100%	100%	100%	100%	80%	100%	100%	100%	100%	100%	100%	100%

RESERVE AMOUNT NEEDED

ITEM	2012	2013	2014	2015	2016	2017	2018	2019	2020	2021	2022	2023	2024	2025
FENCES	50,000	25,000	-	-	-	-	-	-	-	-	-	-	-	-
LIGHTING	-	52,000	-	-	-	-	-	-	-	-	-	-	-	-
RETAINING WALLS	-	-	86,250	-	-	-	-	-	-	-	-	-	-	-
ROADS	-	-	-	140,000	210,000	-	-	-	-	-	-	-	-	-
CURBS/SIDEWALKS	-	-	-	52,500	87,500	-	-	-	-	-	-	-	-	-
CLUBHOUSE/POOL/TENNIS	-	15,000	-	-	-	-	-	-	-	-	-	-	-	-
ROOF	-	-	-	-	-	-	-	-	-	350,000	350,000	-	525,000	525,000
PAINTING	35,000	245,000	245,000	-	-	-	-	-	-	-	-	-	-	-
IRRIGATION	-	-	-	-	-	-	-	-	-	-	-	-	-	-
TOTAL	85,000	337,000	331,250	192,500	297,500	-	-	-	-	350,000	350,000	-	525,000	525,000

236 A FRAMEWORK FOR HOA MANAGEMENT

extensions to the basic capital budget spreadsheet.

If a board member has a background in basic finance, the spreadsheet can also show the present value of an annuity for each expected outlay. In simple terms, this is the amount of money that would need to be invested, starting today, for each year until the project begins to meet the expected outlay.

If the amounts involved are substantial or the interest rate environment more normal, allowance should be made for interest received on reserve funds deposited in CDs or similar financial instruments. However, in the current economic climate (circa 2012), deposit rates are so low that interest earned can in most cases be ignored. In addition, in an extremely low interest rate environment, the association is usually better off keeping its investments short term as the returns available do not justify locking funds up for long periods.

The treasurer should take this first draft before the entire board, explaining what assumptions have been made and pointing out any financial trouble spots. Based upon the draft, the board may desire to omit or defer some projects that are superfluous or of low priority. The timing of projects can be adjusted to some extent, but should not be in dramatic disagreement with lifetime estimates provided by the planning report engineer. The treasurer should then update the spreadsheet to generate the final version of the budget. This document should then approved by the board at its next meeting.

The approval of the capital budget must include a caveat that the figures used reflect the board's best estimate of the future needs of the association and that the board reserves the right to modify, as necessary and as it sees fit, the timing, extent and nature of the projects. The final version of the budget, along with a suitable proclamation, should be distributed to the entire membership of the association and filed with the management agency. The association's auditor will use these documents when preparing the annual audited financial statements and include appropriate language to reflect the association's future

Figure 5 Advanced Capital Budget Spread Sheet

AMOUNT TO RESERVE (annually)

ITEM	2012	2013	2014	2015	2016	2017	2018	2019	2020	2021	2022	2023	2024	2025
FENCES	(49,865)	(12,435)	0	0	0	0	0	0	0	0	0	0	0	0
LIGHTING	0	(25,865)	0	0	0	0	0	0	0	0	0	0	0	0
RETAINING WALLS	0	0	(28,419)	0	0	0	0	0	0	0	0	0	0	0
ROADS	0	0	0	(34,291)	(40,942)	0	0	0	0	0	0	0	0	0
CURBS/SIDEWALKS	0	0	0	(12,859)	(17,059)	0	0	0	0	0	0	0	0	0
CLUBHOUSE/POOL/TENNIS	0	(120,597)	(79,794)	0	0	0	0	0	0	0	0	0	0	0
ROOF	0	0	0	0	0	0	0	0	(32,422)	(29,249)	0	0	(34,148)	(31,293)
PAINTING	0	(7,461)	0	0	0	0	0	0	0	0	0	0	0	0
IRRIGATION	(34,905)	0	0	0	0	0	0	0	0	0	0	0	0	0

DUES AND FUND BALANCES

ITEM	2012	2013	2014	2015	2016	2017	2018	2019	2020	2021	2022	2023	2024	2025
Dues	510,000	522,000	528,000	540,000	552,000	564,000	576,000	582,000	593,640	605,513	617,623	629,976	648,000	660,000
Operating costs	319,325	328,905	338,772	348,935	359,403	370,185	381,291	392,729	404,511	416,647	429,146	442,020	455,281	468,940
Reserves contribution	190,675	193,095	189,228	191,065	192,597	193,815	194,709	189,271	189,129	188,866	188,477	187,955	192,719	191,060
Loan	0	0	0	0	0	0	0	0	0	0	0	0	0	0
Loan amortization	0	0	0	0	0	0	0	0	0	0	0	0	0	0
Assessment (per % above)	0	118,000	133,750	82,500	127,500	0	0	0	0	150,000	150,000	0	225,000	225,000
Approx. interest on reserves	1,384	1,657	1,292	945	947	691	1,179	1,655	2,132	2,610	2,212	1,813	2,299	1,470
Total source of funds	192,059	312,753	324,270	274,510	321,044	194,505	195,888	190,926	191,261	341,476	340,689	189,768	420,018	417,531
Use of funds	(85,000)	(455,000)	(465,000)	(275,000)	(425,000)	0	0	0	0	(500,000)	(500,000)	0	(750,000)	(750,000)
Net funds	107,059	(142,247)	(140,730)	(490)	(103,956)	194,505	195,888	190,926	191,261	(158,524)	(159,311)	189,768	(329,982)	(332,469)
Ending cash balance	469,859	327,612	186,882	186,392	82,436	276,941	472,830	663,756	855,017	696,492	537,182	726,950	396,968	64,498
Monty Dues	425	435	440	450	460	470	480	485	495	505	515	525	540	550
Monthly Assessment	0	98	111	69	106	0	0	0	0	125	125	0	188	188

plans. Failure to have any type of capital plan can result in a negative footnote on the association's audited financial statements and may harm the resale values of homes within the association.

Conclusion

THE ESSENTIAL THEME throughout *A Framework for HOA Management* is that the board must treat their fellow homeowners with patience and respect and must actively communicate with them. Hiding in a locked board room will only breed the contempt and resentment of residents, creating a situation where board members are on the defensive by default. Be a *communications* board! By adopting this approach, the board will find there are far fewer confrontations with individuals or groups of homeowners, and the job of managing the association will be that much easier.

The sub-theme is that learning, preparation and planning are essential to the successful management of both capital projects and the day-to-day operation of any association. Board meetings are a waste of time if board members do not think about the agenda items in advance or fail to read the documentation provided to them by the property manager. Board members are not expected to be experts in asphalt, painting or any of the myriad other maintenance and management issues which come before them. However, they should take the time to become familiar with the basics of the matter at hand. *Always ask questions!*

Be proactive. A board that does not plan for the future leaves the association open to financial disaster years later. Management is not just about next week or next month. Two, five, even ten or more years down the road may demand far more attention than this season's landscaping.

Finally, take an interest in the property by walking the grounds and looking at the buildings at least a few times each year. The association can have the best property manager in the world, but board members will always see more as they are looking at their own homes and property. Caring comes from within.

Appendices

Appendix A

Example Policies

Conflict of Interest Policy

A. **Definitions.**

Terms used in this policy are defined below:

1. "Financial Interest" means any monetary benefit and includes any of the following interests:

   a. Either directly or indirectly, or otherwise possessing a financial interest of any nature in or with any company or other entity in any way involved in the subject of a board vote; or

   b. Interests as a party who would financially benefit in the transaction being voted upon; or

   c. Interests as a legal representative of any homeowner, board member or any other party who is the subject of such vote or discussion.

2. "Close personal relations" is a relationship involving a board member's spouse, in-laws, parent(s), (step)children, or sibling(s).

3. "Business relations" means a material business relationship with a board member's employer, partner, co-owner, client, or a supplier.

244   A FRAMEWORK FOR HOA MANAGEMENT

B. **No Financial Benefit.**

    1. No board member or member of their household may receive any financial benefit of any nature, including, but not limited to, money, gifts, or other consideration from any person (including close personal relations) or firm doing business with the association or as the result of transactions involving the association, unless previously disclosed and approved by a the vote of the uninvolved board members.

    2. Attorneys who are board members are not to represent other members of the association.

My signature signifies that I have read this policy and that I understand my responsibilities under the policy.

Signature:

Date signed:

Policy on Dishonesty, Fraud and Suspected Misconduct

The association has risks from wrongdoing, dishonesty, fraud and misconduct. The impact of dishonesty and misconduct can include, but is not limited to:

- The financial loss incurred

- Damaging the reputation of the association or its members

- Negative public relations

- Legal costs

- Reduction in the value of properties

- Relations with contractors or suppliers

The board must manage these risks and their potential impact. The board establishes with this policy an honest, ethical and fair business environment for the association, its members, managing agent, contractors and suppliers.

The board seeks to prevent, detect and correct any dishonesty and misconduct. The discovery and documentation of these acts will be referred to law enforcement agencies as appropriate and necessary.

Coverage. This policy covers all of the association's employees, officers, board members, management agency and vendors.

Definition of Fraud. Fraud is an intentional deception, misappropriation of resources, or the manipulation of data to the disadvantage of the association. Examples of fraud include:

- Falsification of expenses and invoices,

- Theft of cash or other assets,

- Alteration or falsification of records,

- Misappropriation of funds, and

- Knowingly providing false information on financial or other records or documents.

Obligation to Report. All employees, officers, and board members of the association and the managing agent have a duty to report suspicions about the possible fraudulent or corrupt activity of any officer, employee, agent, member, vendor or any other party related to the business of the association. Any person having a reason to believe fraudulent or corrupt acts have occurred has the responsibility to report this information immediately to the president of the board of directors or, if the allegation involves the president, to any other board member.

Whistle Blower Protection. Retaliation and retribution will not be tolerated against any employee, officer, member, or board member who reports suspected fraudulent or corrupt activities. If deemed necessary or appropriate, the association will notify and fully cooperate with the appropriate law enforcement agency.

Corrective Action. Depending upon the seriousness of the offense, action can range from written reprimand from the board of directors up to legal action – either civil or criminal. When monetary losses to the association are involved, the association will seek recovery of losses.

My signature signifies that I have read this policy and that I understand my responsibilities under the policy.

Signature:
Date signed:

Homeowner Insurance Policy

Purpose. To protect the association from the potential loss of its homes, the association's homeowners' agreement obligates homeowners to provide proof of adequate insurance to the association.

Required Terms of Insurance. All homeowners must maintain insurance with the following minimum terms:

1. Customary property and casualty insurance terms insuring the unit against loss by fire or other calamity;

2. Must provide for the full replacement value with no deductions for depreciation;

3. Include at least $1 million of customary liability insurance directly or with supplementary umbrella; and

4. Must name The Pines Home Owners Association, Inc. as an "additional insured" and provide it with notice of changes to the insurance coverage.

Evidence of Insurance.

1. The managing agent will send a notice to homeowners not less than once a year requesting evidence of the required insurance;

2. Homeowners will promptly notify the managing agent of any change to the terms, provisions, or provider of their homeowners' insurance policy and provide a new certificate of insurance on the renewal or modification of their homeowners' insurance policy.

Records and Reporting. The management agent will keep accurate and up-to-date records of all homeowners who have provided evidence of insurance, their compliance with the insurance requirements, the start and expiration dates of the policy, and any and all changes to homeowner insurance policies received by the managing agent. The managing agent will provide reports to the board of directors of the above at each scheduled meeting of the board.

Arrears Policy

Purpose. The homeowners' agreement and bylaws mandate the board of directors to take action as necessary to collect common charges and other assessments. This policy implements these provisions, establishes the uniform treatment of arrearages, and provides for the notification of the policy to homeowners.

Arrearage. Any failure to pay the full amount of the common charges and any assessments authorized by the board of directors.

Actions Upon Failure to Pay. When an arrearage occurs, the board of directors will,

1. Upon an arrearage in an aggregate amount equal to one months' payment of common charges, impose (a) interest at a rate equal to 1.5% per month and (b) a late fee of $40 per month for each month that the arrearage continues;

2. Upon an arrearage in an aggregate amount equal to two months' payment of common charges, direct the managing agent to send a delinquency notice to the homeowner;

3. Upon an arrearage in an aggregate amount equal to three months' payment of common charges, suspend the homeowner's right to use common facilities and services and refer the matter to the Legal Subcommittee;

4. Upon an arrearage in an aggregate amount equal to four months' payment of common charges, direct the association's attorney to advise the homeowner of the association's intention to pursue legal remedies, including the imposition of a lien, unless such charges are paid within 30 days;

5. Upon an arrearage in an aggregate amount equal to six months' payment of common charges direct the association's attorneys to file a notice of lien; and

6. Upon an arrearage in an aggregate amount equal to nine months' payment of common charges, direct the association's attorneys to commence an appropriate action to collect or foreclose upon the lien granted to the association.

Expenses Related to Collection. All fees and expenses, including attorneys, incurred by the association in collecting an arrearage will be charged to the homeowner and added to the homeowner's common charges.

No Limitations. The remedies set forth in this policy do not limit any actions available to the association under the homeowners' agreement or the bylaws or the ability of the board to negotiate agreements on a case-by-case basis with individual homeowners regarding arrearages and the terms thereof.

Notification of Policy. This policy shall be placed in the residents' manual distributed to homeowners, but the failure to distribute this policy to any homeowner will not constitute or be deemed to be a waiver of the right to take the actions listed in the policy.

Contracting Procedures Policy

Purpose. This policy establishes guidelines for selecting and contracting with vendors and service providers so as to ensure that the association gets good value for all of its contracted goods and services.

General. All contracts relating to capital expenditures, more than one year in length, or with aggregate expenditures in excess of $50,000 are to be by competitive bid, except in the case of an emergency during which the board determines competitive bidding to be impracticable. At least three proposal should be obtained for all contracts.

Requests for Proposal. Prior to the selection of any provider of goods and services likely to exceed $50,000 in value or more than one year in length, the managing agent must prepare, subject to prior approval by the board of directors, a Request for Proposal, containing all necessary information about the goods to be purchased or the work to be performed, including

- a complete and accurate description of the goods to be purchased or the work to be performed;

- time constraints for submitting a bid, commencing and completing services;

- qualifications of the prospective bidders as specified below;

- acceptable days and hours for any work to be performed or goods to be delivered;

- any unique specifications or special conditions;

- requirements for the submission of proposals;

- requirements for final completion of the work;

- requiring the compliance with all laws and regulations related to the work to be performed or goods to be purchased; and

- requiring the disclosure of all subcontractors.

The Request for Proposal should be submitted to at least three vendors or contractors that have been identified as capable of providing the goods or services requested and may reasonably be expected to satisfy the qualifications described in this policy or in the Request for Proposal.

Requirements for the Submission of Proposals. All proposals submitted must include

- a schedule of the work to be done or of the delivery of goods;

- all applicable taxes, performance bonds and permits;

- any available discounts;

- a list of all subcontractors (subject to the approval of the association); and

- at least five references.

Qualifications. All providers of goods or services to the association, including all subcontractors, must

1. be fully licensed and bonded to the extent required by law;

2. be properly organized and recognized, if a corporation, limited liability company, limited partnership, or other similar legal entity;

3. be licensed to do business in Plains County, if operating under an assumed name (i.e., "DBA");

4. provide proof of adequate liability insurance and workers' compensation through the completion of the contract; and

5. have net assets and free cash sufficient to meet all of their obligations to the association.

Before approving and delivering any contract subject to the terms of this policy, the board will review proof of the qualifications of the provider.

Payments. Unless the board of directors determines that such payment terms are impracticable or unavailable, (a) no more than 25% deposited as a down payment and (b) a retention of 30% will be withheld of the total payment until completion is finalized. Final completion is when (i) all discrepancies have been corrected, (ii) a final walk through has been made by the contractor and the association or its representative, and (iii) the contractor, subcontractors, and suppliers have all provided a written waiver of liens to the association and its managing agent.

Acceptance of a Proposal. Before signing a contract for any goods and services, the board of directors will, with due diligence, consider each timely delivered proposal. In considering each of the bids, the board will take into account not only the costs, but also the quality of the goods or services provided, the qualifications of the bidders, and any other qualities the board deems appropriate to consideration of the bids.

Notice to Homeowners. At least 10 days prior to approving a proposed contract for goods or services anticipated to exceed $50,000 in total value or more than one year in length, the board of directors will provide notice to homeowners of the principal terms of the proposed contract and the opportunity for homeowners to review and comment on the proposed contract. Such notice may be giving in writing or orally at a public meeting of the board of directors if also supplemented by notices displayed in common areas. Financing, if not by the use of reserves or assessment, must also be disclosed.

Cost Overruns. All changes in the cost of a signed contract must be approved by the board of directors.

Appendix B

The Monthly Report

ON THE FOLLOWING PAGES ARE sample reports a board member can expect to find within the monthly financial report prepared by the management agency. The complete report can be quite lengthy and is largely dependent upon how many units are in the association. Every management agent has their own take on what data to include and how to format it; the reports included here should be common to any association.

Not shown here are copies of bank statements, correspondence to owners and contractors, and other special reports, such as an insurance compliance or homeowner complaint log. Always make sure that a copy of the banking statements are included in the complete report. Doing so provides another level of security as any board member is then able to question suspicious changes in the statements.

An arrears report has not been included as the format and contents are the same as the rent ledger, but only homeowners with outstanding balances are shown on the arrears report. A current arrears report is usually run the day of the board meeting and distributed to all board members.

Unfortunately, all too often board members focus their attention just on the arrears report and do not pay close attention to the profit/loss statement and check listings. This is regrettable as correcting errors or misbooked entries is significantly easier in the month they occur, rather than many months later when someone realizes "something just doesn't look right." Timing considerations may also prove important when evaluating the statements in the monthly report package.

THE PINES HOA
CASH FLOW SUMMARY
OCTOBER 2011

Date: 11/04/2011

Time: 5:12PM

FIRST NATIONAL BANK OPERATING ACCOUNT

OPENING BALANCE 10/1/2011	$	39,853.14

PLUS

INCOME - FROM OWNERS

COMMON CHARGES	$	41,265.00
LEGAL FEES	$	-
INSURANCE CERTIFICATE VIOLATION	$	-
POOL FEES	$	40.00
LATE.NSFCH, INTEREST ON ARREARS	$	323.48
	$	41,628.48

LESS

DISBURSEMENTS BY CHECKS	$	(42,050.56)
DISBURSEMENTS BY EFT- LOAN SERVICE	$	-
TRANSFER TO RESERVE ACCOUNT	$	(18,882.91)
BANK CHARGES- DEPOSIT SLIPS	$	-
BANK CHARGES- SERVICE.NSF FEE	$	-
NYS CORP TAX BY EFT	$	-
CLOSING BAL FIRST NATIONAL CASH ACCT 10/31/2011	$	20,548.15
OUTSTANDING CHECKS/TRANSFERS	$	-
DEPOSIT IN TRANSIT	$	(1,170.00)
CLOSING BAL FIRST NATIONAL OPERATING 10/31/2011	$	19,378.15

RESERVE ACCOUNTS   10/31/2011

NORTHERN FINANCIAL RESERVE ACCOUNT	$	137,218.98
NORTHERN FINANCIAL CHECKING ACCOUNT	$	1,000.00
REGENT RESERVE ACCOUNT	$	78,356.22
REGENT CHECKING ACCOUNT	$	1,000.00
FIRST NATIONAL RESERVE -OPENED BY FOREST MGMT	$	231,448.37

THE PINES HOA	Date: 11/04/2011
Balance Sheet - As of 10/31/2011	Time: 5:12PM

ASSET

Cash In Bank

The Pines HOA First National Oper.	19,378.15	
The Pines Northern Financial Oper.	1,000.00	
The Pines HOA Regent Oper.	1,000.00	
Cash In Bank – Total		21,378.15

Reserve Acct

The Pines HOA M/M First National	231,448.37	
The Pines HOA M/M Northern Financial	137,218.98	
The Pines HOA M/M Regent Bank	78,356.22	
Reserve Acct - Total		447,023.57

ASSET - Total	468,401.72
TOTAL CASH AND FIXED ASSETS	468,401.72

LIABILITY

Liability Toward Homeowners

Prepaid Dues	1,700.00	
Liability Toward Homeowners - Total		1,700.00

LIABILITY – Total

EQUITY

Homeowners Equity

Homeowners Equity	357,046.95	
Homeowners Equity- Total		357,046.95
Current Year Retained Earnings		109,654.77

EQUITY – Total	466,701.72
TOTAL LIABILITIES AND EQUITY	468,401.72

Forest Mgt Co.

THE PINES HOA

Check Listing Report

10/01/2011 – 10/31/2011

Date: 11/04/2011

Time: 5:18PM

Page: 1

Date	ChkNo	Sts	Payee	Description	JrnlID	GL Acct	Amt
10/07/11	348	Paid	VERIZON	555-555-1212	312846	430	30.19
10/07/11	349	Paid	WE CLEAN INC	9/2011 Clean clubhouse	312847	680	165.25
10/07/11	350	Paid	DENISE ROUL CPA	Accounting Services, 10/2011	312848	510	400.00
10/07/11	351	Paid	ALERT SECURITY	Alarm	312849	640	457.33
10/07/11	352	Paid	JAMES LAVICHE	Rekey all common locks	312850	670	408.03
10/07/11	353	Paid	ROSSI ELECTRIC	Fix blown fuse in clubhouse	312851	685	90.00
10/11/11	355	Paid	CIRCLE INDUSTRIES INC	Repave traffic circle	312853	625	1,283.18
10/15/11	356	Paid	PGE	A/C 3910932093091903913	312854	510	227.86
10/15/11	357	Paid	PGE	A/C 0492092845098490382	312855	510	212.77
10/15/11	359	Paid	PGE	A/C 4930498490345223993	312857	550	18.04
10/17/11	360	Paid	ED FITZSIMMONS LLC	Spray birch tree	312858	664	1,391.58
10/20/11	361	Paid	DEEP END MGT	Pool supplies	312859	651	625.66
10/20/11	362	Paid	DEEP END MGT	Pool chemicals	312860	652	318.11
10/23/11	363	Paid	ASSOCIATED WATER	A/C 0000049248010130	312861	415	1,442.18
10/23/11	364	Paid	SHERMAN BUEL & RODGERS	Re: Smith #132	312862	505	185.00
10/23/11	365	Paid	ASSOCIATED WATER	A/C 0000095904039042	312863	415	815.12
10/23/11	366	Paid	ASSOCIATED WATER	A/C 0000023409309211	312864	415	382.12
							8,452.42

The Pines HOA
Rent Roll Report
10/01/2011 – 10/31/2011

Date: 11/04/2011
Time: 5:19PM
Page: 1

	Code	Beginning Balance	Current Charges	Current Payments	Ending Balance
COMMON CHARGES	CND	7,242.00	42,500.00	38,872.00	8,870.00
LATE FEE	LT	2,269.43	350.00	245.00	2,374.43
INTEREST ON BALANCE	INR	9,086.52	624.95	48.62	9,662.85
INSURANCE NON COMPLIANCE	EMS	500.00	200.00	0.00	700.00
RENT IN ARREARS THRU	ARR	15,720.00	0.00	393.00	15,327.00
LEGAL CHARGES	LGL	10,834.11	0.00	0.00	10834.11
REPAIRS	REP	202.21	0.00	0.00	202.21
POOL CHARGES	POOL	124.00	0.00	35.00	89.00
TITLE SEARCH	TIT	319.90	0.00	0.00	319.90
TOTALS		46,298.17	43,674.95	39,593.62	48,379.50

The Pines HOA
Rent Ledger
10/01/2011 – 10/31/2011

Date: 11/04/2011
Time: 5:14PM
Page: 1

UNIT	TENANT NAME	CODE	BEG. BAL	CUR. BAL	CUR. PMTS.	END BAL.	LAST PMT	NEXT DUE
001	ANNE CHOW	CND	0.00	425.00	425.00	0.00	11/03/11	12/01/11
			0.00	425.00	405.00	0.00		
002	CHRISTINE VALENTA	CND	-425.00	425.00	0.00	0.00	11/03/11	12/01/11
			-425.00	425.00	0.00	0.00		
003	FRED NOWLEN	CND	0.00	425.00	425.00	0.00	11/03/11	12/01/11
			0.00	425.00	425.00	0.00		
004	OSCAR DEJESUS	CND	0.00	425.00	425.00	0.00	10/13/11	12/01/11
			0.00	425.00	425.00	0.00		
005	LAWRENCE KIND	CND	0.00	425.00	425.00	0.00	11/03/11	12/01/11
			0.00	425.00	425.00	0.00		
006	HEIRNY FLUFFENDUD	CND	0.00	425.00	425.00	0.00	10/05/11	12/01/11
			0.00	425.00	425.00	0.00		
007	JILL RUYBAL	CND	0.00	425.00	425.00	0.00	10/06/11	12/01/11
		LT	40.00	0.00	40.00	0.00		
		INK	6.08	0.00	6.08	0.00		
			46.08	425.00	471.08	0.00		
008	TYRONE UMANA	CND	0.00	425.00	425.00	0.00	10/04/11	12/01/11
			0.00	425.00	425.00	0.00		

The Pines HOA
Rent Ledger
10/01/2011 – 10/31/2011

Date: 11/04/2011
Time: 5:14PM
Page: 2

UNIT	TENANT NAME	CODE	BEG. BAL	CUR. BAL	CUR. PMTS	END BAL	LAST PMT	NEXT DUE
		ARR	13,723.00	0.00	0.00	13,723.00		
		LT	1,320.00	40.00	0.00	1,360.00		
		INR	7,985.57	399.28	0.00	8,384.85		
		LGL	6,814.18	0.00	0.00	6,814.18		
		REP	418.39	0.00	0.00	418.39		
		CND	4,250	425.00	0.00	4,675.00		
		ADCC	18.00	0.00	0.00	18.00		
009	ALTHEA KIVI	INS	0.00	75.00	0.00	75.00	--none--	12/01/11
			34,529.14	939.28	0.00	35,468.42		
010	LAWRENCE KIND	CND	0.00	425.00	425.00	0.00	11/03/11	12/01/11
			0.00	425.00	425.00	0.00		
011	LUCILLE VAVOOM	CND	0.00	425.00	425.00	0.00	10/05/11	12/01/11
		CND	0.00	425.00	425.00	0.00		
		LT	0.00	450.00	425.00	25.00		
		INK	40.00	0.00	40.00	0.00		
012	JENNIFER BEEDLESAT		6.08	0.00	6.08	0.00	10/06/11	12/01/11
			46.08	450.00	471.08	25.00		
013	HERMAN FREEZE	CND	-425.00	425.00	425.00	-425.00	10/04/11	12/01/11
			-425.00	425.00	425.00	-425.00		

The Pines HOA
Profit/Loss Statement
Through October 2011

Date: 11/04/2011
Time: 5:12PM

Acct ID	Description	Actual Month	Budget Month	% Bdgt. Used	YTD Actual	YTD Budget	% YTD Bdgt Used	Annual Budget	% Annual Bdgt. Used
INCOME									
300	COMMON CHARGE INCOME	41,265.00	42,500.00	97.09	411,318.53	425,000.00	96.78	510,000.00	80.65
310	INTEREST ON RESERVE ACCTS	46.51	60.00	77.52	566.19	600.00	94.37	720.00	78.64
316	ASSESSMENT (FENCE)	0.00	0.00	0.00	33,600.00	35,000.00	96.00	35,000.00	96.00
318	ASSESMENT (PAINT)	0.00	0.00	0.00	0.00	0.00	0.00	0.00	0.00
330	POOL INCOME	40.00	0.00	0.00	96.00	200.00	48.00	200.00	48.00
340	OTHER INCOME	323.48	0.00	0.00	1,103.78	0.00	0.00	0.00	0.00
370	CLUBHOUSE RENTAL	0.00	0.00	0.00	0.00	0.00	0.00	0.00	0.00
	TOTAL INCOME	41,674.99	42,560.00	97.92	446,684.50	460,800.00	96.94	545,920.00	81.82
EXPENSES									
	ADMINISTRATIVE EXPENSES								
505	ATTORNEY FEES	185.00	541.67	34.15	5,790.46	5,416.67	106.90	6,500.00	89.08
510	AUDITOR	400.00	0.00	0.00	3,600.00	3,500.00	102.86	5,000.00	72.00
515	PROFESSIONAL SERVICES	0.00	0.00	0.00	418.55	0.00	0.00	0.00	0.00
520	BANK CHARGES	0.00	0.00	0.00	86.12	0.00	0.00	0.00	0.00

The Pines HOA
Profit/Loss Statement
Through October 2011

Date: 11/04/2011
Time: 5:12PM

Acct ID	Description	Actual Month	Budget Month	% Bdgt. Used	YTD Actual	YTD Budget	% YTD Bdgt Used	Annual Budget	% Annual Bdgt. Used
522	INTERNET SERVICES	0.00	0.00	0.00	375.00	400.00	93.75	400.00	93.75
590	MANAGEMENT AGENT FEE	3,000.00	3,000.00	100.00	30,000.00	30,000.00	100.00	36,000.00	83.33
595	OFFICE	123.12	200.00	61.56	661.79	2,000.00	33.09	2,400.00	27.57
430	TELEPHONE	30.19	29.17	103.51	362.28	291.67	124.21	350.00	103.51
560	EQUIPMENT RENTAL	0.00	0.00	0.00	157.00	200.00	78.50	200.00	78.50
595	MISC. EXPENSES	0.00	62.50	0.00	1,126.59	625.00	180.25	750.00	150.21
	TOTAL ADM EXPENSES	3,738.31	3,833.33	97.52	42,577.79	42,433.33	100.34	51,600.00	82.52
	UTILITIES								
405	ELECTRICITY	917.28	770.83	119.00	6,715.84	7,708.33	87.12	9,250.00	72.60
415	WATER	2,639.42	666.67	395.91	7,921.94	6,666.67	118.83	8,000.00	99.02
420	SEWER	0.00	0.00	0.00	0.00	0.00	0.00	0.00	0.00
425	GAS	32.71	208.33	15.70	1,005.81	2,083.33	48.28	2,500.00	40.23
495	OTHER UTILITIES	0.00	0.00	0.00	0.00	0.00	0.00	0.00	0.00
	TOTAL UTILITIES	3,589.41	1,645.83	218.09	15,643.59	16,458.33	95.05	19,750.00	79.21
	MAINTENANCE AND REPAIRS								
600	GENERAL REPAIRS & MAINT.	922.81	333.33	276.84	5,753.51	3,333.33	172.61	4,000.00	143.84
605	HVAC REPAIRS	0.00	0.00	0.00	383.60	750.00	51.15	750.00	51.15

The Pines HOA
Profit/Loss Statement
Through October 2011

Date: 11/04/2011
Time: 5:12PM

Acct ID	Description	Actual Month	Budget Month	% Bdgt. Used	YTD Actual	YTD Budget	% YTD Bdgt Used	Annual Budget	% Annual Bdgt. Used
610	FURNACE REPAIRS	0.00	0.00	0.00	0.00	750.00	0.00	750.00	0.00
615	PLUMBING	0.00	0.00	0.00	201.80	500.00	40.36	500.00	40.36
620	MASONARY	0.00	0.00	0.00	0.00	2,000.00	0.00	2,000.00	0.00
625	PAVING	1,283.18	0.00	0.00	2,118.55	4,000.00	52.96	4,000.00	52.96
630	FENCES & GATES	0.00	0.00	0.00	0.00	500.00	0.00	500.00	0.00
635	EXTERMINATOR	0.00	0.00	0.00	7,200.00	8,000.00	90.00	9,000.00	80.00
640	LIGHTS/ALARMS	547.33	83.33	656.80	547.33	833.33	65.68	1,000.00	54.73
670	DRAINAGE	0.00	0.00	0.00	1,671.28	3,500.00	47.75	3,500.00	47.75
675	ROOF REPAIRS	0.00	0.00	0.00	3,879.25	5,000.00	77.59	5,000.00	77.59
680	CLUBHOUSE CLEANING	165.25	166.67	99.15	1,776.80	1,666.67	106.61	2,000.00	88.84
685	ELECTRICIAN	90.00	62.50	144.00	325.00	625.00	52.00	750.00	43.33
690	MISC SUPPLIES	105.18	125.00	84.14	511.37	1,250.00	40.91	1,500.00	34.09
695	GOVT. PERMITS	0.00	0.00	0.00	275.00	300.00	91.67	300.00	91.67
	TOTAL REPAIR & MAINT.	3,113.75	770.83	403.95	24,643.49	33,008.33	74.66	35,550.00	69.32
	POOLS TENNIS COURT								
650	POOL MANAGEMENT	0.00	0.00	0.00	24,886.18	24,000.00	103.69	24,000.00	103.69
651	POOL SUPPLIES/REPAIRS	625.66	0.00	0.00	1,712.35	2,500.00	68.49	2,500.00	68.49
652	POOL CHEMICALS	318.11	0.00	0.00	2,915.66	3,500.00	83.30	3,500.00	83.30

The Pines HOA
Profit/Loss Statement
Through October 2011

Date: 11/04/2011
Time: 5:12PM

Acct ID	Description	Actual Month	Budget Month	% Bdgt. Used	YTD Actual	YTD Budget	% YTD Bdgt Used	Annual Budget	% Annual Bdgt. Used
655	TENNIS COURT MAINT	0.00	0.00	0.00	4,315.28	3,250.00	132.78	3,250.00	132.78
	TOTAL POOL & TENNIS COURTS	943.77	0.00	0.00	33,829.47	33,250.00	101.74	33,250.00	101.74
	GROUNDS								
660	LANDSCAPE CONTRACT	10,078.13	10,000.00	100.78	109,674.32	100,000.00	109.67	120,000.00	91.40
661	COMMON FLOWERS/PLANTS	485.88	0.00	0.00	2,753.11	3,600.00	76.48	3,600.00	76.48
663	TREES (NEW)	0.00	0.00	0.00	2,625.00	5,000.00	52.50	5,000.00	52.50
664	TREES (PRUNING)	0.00	7,500.00	0.00	9,888.37	17,500.00	56.50	17,500.00	56.50
665	IRRIGATION	281.66	500.00	56.33	3,184.48	3,000.00	106.15	3,000.00	106.15
668	STORM RESERVE	0.00	1,000.00	0.00	1,623.66	4,000.00	40.59	6,000.00	27.06
669	SNOW PLOW/SALT/SAND	0.00	0.00	0.00	9,123.56	6,000.00	152.06	10,000.00	91.24
	TOTAL GROUNDS	10,845.67	19,000.00	57.08	138,872.50	139,100.00	99.84	165,100.00	84.11
	GENERAL EXPENSES								
705	INTEREST ON LOANS	0.00	0.00	0.00	226.88	225.00	100.84	225.00	100.84
710	CORPORATE TAX	0.00	0.00	0.00	685.00	750.00	91.33	750.00	91.33
715	INSURANCE	0.00	0.00	0.00	4,190.65	4,537.50	92.36	5,500.00	76.19
720	WORKER COMP INS	0.00	0.00	0.00	68.20	100.00	68.20	100.00	68.20

The Pines HOA
Profit/Loss Statement
Through October 2011

Date: 11/04/2011
Time: 5:12PM

Acct ID	Description	Actual Month	Budget Month	% Bdgt. Used	YTD Actual	YTD Budget	% YTD Bdgt Used	Annual Budget	% Annual Bdgt. Used
725	DISABILITY INS	0.00	0.00	0.00	444.50	500.00	88.90	500.00	88.90
740	INSURANCE CLAIMS	0.00	0.00	0.00	0.00	0.00	0.00	0.00	0.00
790	OPER. RESERVE	0.00	0.00	0.00	0.00	7,000.00	0.00	7,000.00	0.00
	TOTAL GENERAL EXPENSES	0.00	0.00	0.00	5,615.23	13,112.50	42.82	14,075.00	39.90
	TOTAL OPERATING EXPENSES	22,230.91	25,250.00	88.04	261,182.07	277,362.50	94.17	319,325.00	81.79
	CAPITAL IMPROVEMENTS								
800	FENCE/GATES	16,000.00	0.00	0.00	48,588.23	70,000.00	69.41	70,000.00	69.41
805	PAINTING(INTERIOR)	0.00	0.00	0.00	1,182.50	3,000.00	39.42	3,000.00	39.42
810	LANDSCAPING PROJECT	0.00	0.00	0.00	2,300.00	1,500.00	153.33	1,500.00	153.33
820	MAILBOXES	3,819.65	0.00	0.00	3,819.65	4,000.00	95.49	4,000.00	95.49
830	CLUBHOUSE	0.00	0.00	0.00	7,615.38	4,500.00	169.23	4,500.00	169.23
	TOTAL CAPITAL IMPROVMENTS	19,819.65	0.00	0.00	63,505.76	83,000.00	76.51	83,000.00	76.51
	PRINCIPAL LOAN PAYMENT	0.00	0.00	0.00	16,474.16	16,000.00	102.96	16,000.00	102.96
	TOTAL EXPENSES	42,050.56	25,250.00	166.54	341,161.99	376,362.50	90.65	418,325.00	81.55
	NET PROFIT (LOSS)	-375.57	17,310.00	-2.17	105,522.51	84,437.50	124.97	127,595.00	82.70
210	TRANSFERS TO RESERVE ACCTS	18,882.91	18,882.91	100.00	188,829.17	188,829.17	100.00	226,595.00	83.33

Appendix C

Outline of a Painting Project

A PAINTING PROJECT IS FAR MORE INVOLVED than selecting a color and hiring a painter to put it on the buildings. To be successful, a considerable amount of preparation by the board and property manager is necessary. On the following pages are a series of "Gantt" charts that outline a painting project at the mythical Pines HOA – twelve buildings, each of six connected town homes. In their simplest form, Gantt charts take tasks and place them on a time-line which provides an easier to understand visual presentation of the project. That is the approach used for the Pines Project. Software to make these charts is widely available, some free, and the association's management agency may have their own preferred program. Often the charts can be updated to reflect the degree of completion of each task, define dependencies between tasks, and even attach costs and personnel resources to each segment. These charts can also be made using a word processor, spread sheet or even by hand, though using software specifically designed to generate Gantt charts provides the best results.

Keep in mind that the charts and general procedures of the painting project can be applied to any other significant capital project, such as paving or roof replacement.

In reviewing the charts, it may be surprising that the project takes so long to complete. Unfortunately, that is often the case with capital projects. The initial portion of the outline depicts those elements directly related to the board and property manager. Though it may be possible to shave a few days off here and there, the reality is that much of the time is spent waiting on others to respond or act.

The committee to find the painters is also involved in defining the requirements for the RFP. This is not as simple as saying "We have 72 homes which need to be painted, how much will that cost?" The RFP must define the scope of work precisely if the bidders are to offer an accurate price. What will be sanded? What will be power washed? Are gutters and leaders to be removed? Must they be replaced each night? Will there be one or two prime coats? Are decks, sheds or other accessories to be included in the scope of work? What days may the painters work? What is the preferred start date? Who will do the required carpentry work? Those are but a few points that the board and property manager must answer prior to sending out an RFP.

Once the RFP goes out, the painters will wish to visit the site. This requires proper scheduling as each contractor should be accompanied by the property manager or a knowledgeable board member who can answer questions about the buildings and the property. Among other things, this is an opportunity for the board to get feedback from the painters on the state of the buildings. It is possible something was overlooked and not included in the RFP or the condition of the buildings may be worse (or better) than was assumed. The board may then send a modified request to all involved.

The association's attorney will need to review any contract proposal and include (or delete) language as necessary to protect the association. This, too, involves back and forth and will take time to complete.

The start date for the actual on-site work is also dependent upon each painter's current schedule. When the board is evaluating the bids, the availability of each painter may affect the ultimate decision of whom to award the job as the size of the project and future weather conditions may preclude waiting for a slightly preferred contractor to be available.

Prior to the start of any work, the board and property manager should hold a special homeowners meeting to discuss the project. This meeting should present the time line of the project, what is required and expected of the homeowners and provide a forum to answer their questions or concerns. Once the painters are on-site, the property manager must keep up with the task of notifying homeowners at the appropriate time of their responsibilities to do repair work. They must also monitor homeowner compliance. A fair portion of the project can run in parallel: when one building is being primed and painted another will be undergoing repair or other preparatory work. A slip-up in completing the preparation work on time for any one building can have a ripple effect that significantly delays other work.

Punch-lists of work that was missed or not done correctly should be developed in conjunction with the painter or their foreman, the property manager and at least one board member. Remember, the people who will pay the most attention to the appearance of the homes are those who live in them. An item which your property manager might miss or not consider a flaw may be one in the eyes of a board member. Punch lists should be made and completed fairly close to when the painter has finished a particular segment of work. Besides keeping the the final review to a manageable size, completion of punch lists can be linked to progress payments to the contractor.

Finally, allowances *must* be made for weather when generating a project time line. If the painter believes that it takes 5 days to prime or paint each building, expect the real figure to be closer to 10 days as rain and excessive heat can cause work stoppages. Weather is a funny thing and often seems to conspire against whatever time constraints are built into a project. It is far easier to accelerate a schedule due to good weather conditions than to extend one which has little room for delays.

Because of this, any project started in the late summer in a colder climate, with an estimated completion of late October or beyond, must have a fall back plan for the shut down of work and completion of the project the following spring. Like rain, cold weather can come early some years, and certainly an abnormally warm fall should not be counted upon. In most cases, paint can be safely applied so long as the temperature will remain above 40 degrees for at least the next four hours. When painting in cold weather, always consult with the manufacturer's local representative to determine the lowest temperature consistent with their warranty.

If a project must be shutdown, all new and repaired wood should be primed and caulked to prevent weather damage over the winter months. The start date for the completion of the project is impossible to predict precisely. Be sure to include a general time frame in the original contract where other provisions for a shut down prior to completion are discussed.

Pines Painting Project 2012
Page 1 of 4

4/1/12

Name	2012 (May–November)	Percent Complet
Board Approves Painting Project		0%
SubCommittee to find local painters		0%
Prepare Painting RFP		0%
Send RFP/Schedule Site Visits		0%
Board Review of RFPs		0%
Interview top two choices		0%
Board Selects Painter		0%
Create procedures for homeowners		0%
Contract Negotiations/Approva		0%
Homeowners meetings		0%
Bldg 1-3		0%
Bldg 1-3 Powerwash		0%
Bldg 1-3 Mark Bad Wood		0%

Summary   Baseline   Summary   Baseline   Current Plan   Baseline

Pines Painting Project 2012

Page 2 of 4

4/1/12

Name	2012							Percent Complet
	May	June	July	August	September	October	November	
Bldg 1-3 Homeowner Repairs				▽ Bldg 1-3 Homeowner Repairs ▽				○ 0%
Bldg 1-3 Sand/Prep				▽ Bldg 1-3 Sand/Prep ▽				○ 0%
Bldg 1-3 Prime				▽ Bldg 1-3 Prime ▽				○ 0%
Bldg 1-3 Finish Coat				Build 1-3 Finish Coat ▽				○ 0%
Bldg 4-6								○ 0%
Bldg 4-6 Powerwash				▽ Bldg 4-6 Powerwash ▽				○ 0%
Bldg 4-6 Mark Bad Wood				Bldg 4-6 Mark Bad Wood ▽				○ 0%
Bldg 4-6 Homeowner Repairs				Bldg 4-6 Homeowner Repairs ▽				○ 0%
Bldg 4-6 Sand/Prep				Bldg 4-6 Sand/Prep ▽				○ 0%
Bldg 4-6 Prime					Bldg 4-6 Prime ▽			○ 0%
Bldg 4-6 Finish Coat					Bldg 4-6 Finish Coat ▽			○ 0%

Summary

Baseline Summary

▽ Current Plan

Baseline

Milestone Professional Trial Version (http://www.kidasa.com)

Pines Painting Project 2012

Page 3 of 4

4/1/12

Name	2012								Percent Complet
	May	June	July	August	September	October	November		
Bldg 7-9								0%
Bldg 7-9 Powerwash				Bldg 7-9 Powerwash				0%
Bldg 7-9 Mark Bad Wood				Bldg 7-9 Mark Bad Wood				0%
Bldg 7-9 Homeowner Repairs				Bldg 7-9 Homeowner Repairs				0%
Bldg 7-9 Sand/Prep					Bldg 7-9 Sand/Prep			0%
Bldg 7-9 Prime					Bldg 7-9 Prime			0%
Bldg 7-9 Finish Coat						Bldg 7-9 Finish Coat		0%
Bldg 10-12								0%
Bldg 10-12 Powerwash					Bldg 10-12 Powerwash			0%
Bldg 10-12 Mark Bad Wood					Bldg 10-12 Mark Bad Wood			0%
Bldg 10-12 Homeowner Repairs					Bldg 10-12 Homeowner Repairs			0%

Summary   Baseline Summary   Current Plan   Baseline

Pines Painting Project 2012

Page 4 of 4   4/1/12

Name	2012							Percent Complet.
	May	June	July	August	September	October	November	
Bldg 10-12 Sand/Prep						Bldg 10-12 Sand/Prep		0%
Bldg 10-12 Prime						Bldg 10-12 Prime		0%
Bldg 10-12 Finish Coat						Bldg 10-12 Finish Coat		0%
Bldg 1-3 Make Punchlist								0%
Bldg 1-3 Do Punchlist						Bldg 1-3 Do Punchlist		0%
Bldg 4-6 Make Punchlist								0%
Bldg 4-6 Do Punchlist						Bldg 4-6 Do Punchlist		0%
Bldg 7-9 Make Punchlist								0%
Bldg 7-9 Do Punchlist							Bldg 7-9 Do Punchlist	0%
Bldg 10-12 Make Punchlist								0%
Bldg 10-12 Do Punchlist							Bldg 10-12 Do Punchlist	0%
Final Checkout							Final Checkout	0%

Summary   Baseline   Summary   Current Plan   Baseline

Appendix D

Electronic Communications

ADVANCES IN COMPUTING AND NETWORKING TECHNOLOGY now allow virtually any person to communicate with any other across the globe instantaneously. What ten years ago was considered a high end computer is now available as a phone that fits in your pants pocket. The "web" enables one to publish their thoughts for anyone on the planet to read.

For the board of an HOA, these technologies offer ways to simplify the management of the property as well as to keep the homeowners better informed and facilitate three-way communication between the property manager, the board and the homeowners.

Throughout this book, reference was made to board discussions carried out by e-mail and the possibility of electronic voting on proposals was also raised. Most board members are probably already familiar with e-mail and many will have access to the Internet through their place of work or home. To operate efficiently, all board members should be prepared to do at least some of the board's business electronically. Accommodations can be made if there is a member with no Internet connection by using the access provided at a public library or that of a friend or neighbor.

Services to Avoid

The first and last rule of using e-mail while on the board is: *no communications related to the association should ever take place through a **personal** e-mail account.* Beyond the obvious issue of mixing business with pleasure, e-mail is *discoverable.* This means that the association must be able to produce e-mail conversations that are relevant to the adjudication of a lawsuit. Personal e-mail accounts do not provide for back-ups and often are the target of hacking and other malfeasance that can result in the user being "locked-out" of their account forever. Clearly, these risks are unacceptable in a corporate environment.

The second rule of e-mail is: *the board should maintain control over this asset.* Many management agencies now offer to provide e-mail and web-hosting services to their HOA clients. Even though this may be the easiest alternative available, it is fraught with risks. To start, by allowing the management agency to setup and operate an e-mail system on the association's behalf, the board is taking the risk that employees of the management agency will read board e-mails, send or receive e-mail using a board member's account, and possibly engage in other unethical acts. Though many board members may believe such actions are unlikely, they must also remember that snooping can be done without their knowledge. The temptation for the property manager and their superiors to eavesdrop if there are "issues" with your account will be extremely high, especially if they believe the board is considering an agent change. It also does not take too much research to discover that not all management agencies are scrupulous, and many a board are caught by surprise when fraud and other illegal activities are discovered. Access to the association's e-mail system and accounts can provide cover cover for, and assist in, committing fraud and other criminal acts.

Another reason not to rely upon the management agency is that all e-mail must be transferable, along with the other records of the association, if a time comes when the board decides to switch agents. Who owns these e-mails? Has your management agent provided a binding legal document that in no uncertain terms states that the association is the owner of any and all content hosted on the management agent's computer systems and networks? If not, you will be relying upon the former agent's good will and professionalism (which may be in doubt if the board is switching agents) to accurately and completely transfer all e-mail and other electronic content. Is the board prepared to sue and pay legal fees if they do not?

A final reason to be wary of services provided by the management agent is that the board has no way of knowing if the system is secure, that procedures are in place to address security exploits as they are published, or that complete and regular back-ups are taken and kept off-site in a secure location. Is the board prepared to hear that a server crash has resulted in the loss of all e-mail history for the association?

Social media, like Facebook or Twitter, are also unacceptable for board level communications since posts, messages and tweets can be permanently deleted as no archival records are maintained. Due to generational issues, social media platforms are less than ideal solutions for communication with homeowners. The need to create a separate account and user profile with the service may also raise privacy concerns for some homeowners. In the future, however, as adoption of social media by older individuals grows, its use as a substitute for a stand alone web page will be more attractive.

Domain Registration

For all the above reasons, the board should instead take steps on their own to setup an e-mail or web hosting environment with one of the many companies on the Internet providing such services. The initial setup of an e-mail only system is not complex, and most firms will provide live assistance and on-line videos to explain the procedure.

The first step the board needs to take is to register a "domain name" for the association. A domain name is used for identification purposes and should already be familiar to any Internet user; names like ibm.com, google.com, att.net are domain names. Corporations typically use the ".com" hierarchy, though as many firms have similar names, some have to register in the ".org," ".net," or another "top-level" domain if the name they wish to use in .com is already taken. The board should try to stay within the .com structure as it is the most familiar to Internet users and often is omitted when names of websites are discussed. If the desired name is taken, for instance thepines.com, consider alternatives like pineshoa.com and similar before trying other top-level domains, such as .org.

The initial availability of a domain name can be checked at `http://www.internic.net/whois.html` or with hosting companies including bluehost.com, eleven2.com, godaddy.com and zoho.com, all of whom can provide e-mail, web and other hosted services. The cost of a domain name is approximately $10 per year, and multi-year registrations are possible.

When registering a domain, information must be given identifying the owner, technical and administrative contacts. The association, *not* a board member, should always be given as the owner. A board member or the property manager may be listed for the technical and administrative contacts – in practice, these contacts are rarely used. Many domain registrars will also offer a "privacy" option which, like an unlisted phone number, limits the details displayed in a public domain name search to a minimum and will not divulge any personal information.

E-mail Only or Complete Hosting Package?

The next decision is whether to select an e-mail only service or a complete web hosting environment. For example, Zoho.com offers Zoho Mail, a sophisticated e-mail service, for about $24 per user, per year. The setup is simple and the user can access mail and calendars from a web browser or a mobile phone.

The term "web hosting" is a bit of a misnomer as it implies that the only use of a web hosting agreement is to maintain an Internet web site, such as www.yahoo.com. In fact, most allow for many additional services, such as e-mail or file storage, and there is never any need to produce any type of web site. The cost is $10 – $20 a month and the fee is all inclusive; there is no per user fee. The interface used to setup the many available functions may appear more daunting to the novice end user than that used by an e-mail only provider, but the actual steps to activate the e-mail function and initialize user accounts is very similar. Again, most providers will have help documentation, videos and live-chat support representatives available to assist in this process. E-mail is accessible through a dedicated web interface as well as by mobile devices.

As the dollar cost is comparable, the decision of which to use really comes down to whether the board envisions creating a simple web site for the association or possibly using a file server to keep board and other documents. If the latter are not desired or are only a distant possibility, using a dedicated e-mail solution is probably the best alternative. If, at some later time the board wishes to explore the other options, there is no difficulty in dropping the e-mail only service and taking on a web hosting agreement. The association owns its domain name for the entire registration period and may use it with any hosting or other service provider.

On Passwords and Account Names

Let there be no mistake: security is essential in the Internet environment. This means that passwords should **not** be common names or number combinations. Even though a password is encrypted, if it is a simple name like "barbara," a sports team like "yankees," or some easy combination like "12345678," hackers will be able to decipher it and access the account. This does not mean passwords must be complete nonsense to be secure – there is something to be said for being able to remember the password without writing it on paper. Taking the prior examples, "bar15bara80" would be a good password and easily remember by Barbara whose birthday is on the 15th of the month in the year 1980. In a similar manner, "yan++kees" is not too hard to remember but is better protected against attack.

The most critical password is the one used by the board member administrating the e-mail or web host service. A backup copy should be given in a sealed envelope to one of the officers whenever the password is changed. This ensures that there will *always* be two board members with access to the control account should something happen to the member responsible for the system.

E-mail account names should follow the corporate standard format first.last@hostname, e.g., bob.jones@thepines.com. Once board member accounts are created, an additional account should be made. The account is for internal only board use, e.g., theboard@thepines.com. All e-mail systems have the ability to set up "forwarders" to redirect or copy e-mail to another user(s). In the case of the board address, a forwarder is set-up to redirect a copy to each board member's e-mail address. To be clear, any mail sent to theboard@thepines.com would then be automatically copied and sent to each board member. Although a group "cc" would accomplish the same thing, the forwarder has the advantage of leaving a permanent copy of the e-mail in the mailbox account theboard@thepines.com and will remain even if individual board members delete their own copy. It is also easier to remember one address instead of several board member names. This is very convenient for both the property manager and officers to communicate with the entire board.

Remember to keep the internal board e-mail address private. If desired, an external address, such as board@thepines.com, can be setup in similar fashion for use by homeowners, residents or other outsiders,

Ideally, a forwarder called file@thepines.com should also be set up to copy the incoming messages sent to each board member into one central location. Unfortunately, making a copy of outgoing mail is beyond the ability of most easily configured e-mail systems. Board members can, however, be asked to cc: the file account on all outgoing communications.

The file account provides security against accidental or even the intentional deletion of board communications. If a lawsuit is filed and copies of e-mail are requested during discovery, the association will be able to provide them and indicate to the court they have taken all available and reasonable precautions to retain the messages. This may be critical if the association itself initiates a legal action and need copies of past e-mails to prove its case.

Web Site, File Servers, Mailing Lists

When using a web hosting account, configuration is done from a secure, administrative web page interface (often called CPanel). Beyond functions to create e-mail accounts, backups and other administrative tasks, some will allow for installation of additional software onto the server. Two popular software installers are Softalicious and Fantastico. Under the "blog" section are a number of appropriate choices for creating a simple web site for the association – one of the most widely used is called "Word-Press." In all cases, with a few mouse clicks the software will be installed and initial administrative usernames and passwords created. From there, minor additional configuration can be done to name the web site or select one of the many "templates" that control the look and feel of a web site.

All blog software functions in a similar way – categories are defined, say board, grounds and pool in the case of an association – and then "posts" are made with the message the board wishes to convey. An example is a post made under the category "pool," with title "Pool Opens Memorial Day" and the content related to pool hours, rules, etc. Once the details are entered and proofread, a mouse click will save the post and it will appear on the front page of the website. Photos can also be included in posts. In some cases, posts may even be made by sending an e-mail to a special address.

It is possible, though not necessary, to do a lot of customization and have a web site which looks beautiful and unlike any other on the Internet. For most associations, a very small amount of customization is more than sufficient, but if one of the board members is interested, or perhaps a "computer person," by all means explore the possibilities!

The board may have no intention of providing updates to the homeowners and only desire a web page with static content. This page is used more as an advertisement or reference for the association. Photos, directions, basic information and perhaps some rules and regulations are all that will appear. Though limited, this type of resource is still valuable as it can assist prospective buyers seeking information on the potential purchase of a home within the association.

File servers, like the name implies, are just simple repositories to keep documents in one place for easy access by all board members. The interfaces are usually designed to look familiar to any Windows or Mac user and are, for all intents, self-explanatory. It is possible to configure different usernames and passwords for different sections of the file server, for instance if the board wished to make some documents available to homeowners while keeping others private. A file server is a good place to keep copies of protocols, contracts, reports, etc. It is *not* a good place to store documents which may divulge personal information that is best kept private.

Mailing list software is also available and may be a good alternative for an association that wishes to keep the homeowners informed in a timely manner, but does not have a board member who feels comfortable working with a blog (or the additional time commitment). Once a mailing list is installed, instructions can be given to the homeowners on how to join the list. This is almost always done by sending an e-mail to the mailing list server (likewise for requests to unsubscribe). When the board has information they wish to convey, they direct a message to a predefined e-mail address, and the server takes care of distributing the message to all members on the list. Some mailing lists can be configured to accept pdf documents and photos. If given permission by the board, the property manager may also use the mailing list to send messages to the homeowners subscribed to the list.

External Assistance

The board may elect to hire an outside consultant to arrange and setup the services described in the above sections. This may be the best solution when the board has no individual who is at all comfortable with computers and networking; though not individually complex, when taken as a whole the steps described may seem overwhelming to a computer novice. Although a consultant can do much of the necessary work, someone from the board must still be available to learn how to change passwords and verify certain administrative details.

Most towns will have at least a few individuals available for hire to assist in setting up domains, e-mail, hosting and create web sites. The competency level to bring the association up to speed is not especially high, so the board should not be too concerned if one candidate is a 19 year old college student. Registering a domain, activating a hosting environment and setting up simple e-mail service should only take a few hours time. Additional time will be required to create a website and the cost will depend greatly on the complexity desired. A simple static web page should take no more than an hour to create once the board provides the written content. A basic Word Press blog, using freely available templates, should not take more than two hours to get up and running. The board may need to contract for additional time to train a member or two in how to post to the website or use a file server.

It is essential that once everything contracted for is in place that at least one, and preferably two, board member(s)) be taught how to change all the administrative passwords. The minimum number of passwords is one (if the domain name is registered with the e-mail/web host provider), but can easily grow to two or more depending on how many additional services beyond basic e-mail are activated. The board must *always* change the administrative passwords to prevent any future unauthorized access by the consultant. In addition, the consultant should verify to the board members that all future billing and owner-ship information has been properly delegated to the association. Annual domain or hosting bills should be directed to the associ-ation's property manager at the management agency, not to the consultant.

The consultant should also demonstrate how to change the password on each e-mail account to the board members. Secu-rity concerns dictate that the final passwords should be entered by a board member and not the consultant. Finally, verify that the only e-mail accounts that have been created are those which the board authorized.

Caveats

A web hosting service allows an association access to e-mail. web pages, file servers, mailing lists, and many other services. However, with each additional service comes the need to have a board member administer that service. In the case of a file server or mailing list, there is usually not much to do after the initial set-up. In the case of a web page ("blog"), there is an additional time commitment. Likewise, if a photo archive is kept online. Care must be taken to be sure the administration and upkeep is not so complex that no other board member has the desire or ability to handle the job. Do not do too much at one time, and make sure everything is working smoothly before adding any additional features.

The author is familiar with, but receives no compensation from any of the companies named in this Appendix. There are many other firms providing the same types of services, and pricing does not vary significantly from vendor to vendor. Always check on the reputation of any firm before engaging their services as uptime, security and user support can vary considerably.

Index

Notes

CPSIA information can be obtained
at www.ICGtesting.com
Printed in the USA
BVHW072343190521
607736BV00002B/270